HOW DO WE KNOW?

An Introduction to Epistemology

JAMES K. DEW JR.
MARK W. FOREMAN

IVP Academic

An imprint of InterVarsity Press
Downers Grove, Illinois

InterVarsity Press
P.O. Box 1400, Downers Grove, IL 60515-1426
World Wide Web: www.ivpress.com
Email: email@ivpress.com

©2014 by James K. Dew Jr. and Mark W. Foreman

All rights reserved. No part of this book may be reproduced in any form without written permission from InterVarsity Press.

InterVarsity Press® is the book-publishing division of InterVarsity Christian Fellowship/USA®, a movement of students and faculty active on campus at hundreds of universities, colleges and schools of nursing in the United States of America, and a member movement of the International Fellowship of Evangelical Students. For information about local and regional activities, write Public Relations Dept., InterVarsity Christian Fellowship/USA, 6400 Schroeder Rd., P.O. Box 7895, Madison, WI 53707-7895, or visit the IVCF website at www.intervarsity.org.

All Scripture quotations, unless otherwise indicated, are taken from the New King James Version®. Copyright © 1982 by Thomas Nelson, Inc. Used by permission. All rights reserved.

Cover design: Cindy Kiple
Interior design: Beth Hagenberg

Image: puzzle piece background: © Liangpv/iStockphoto

ISBN 978-0-8308-4036-6 (print)
ISBN 978-0-8308-6996-1 (digital)

Printed in the United States of America ∞

g green press INITIATIVE *InterVarsity Press is committed to protecting the environment and to the responsible use of natural resources. As a member of Green Press Initiative we use recycled paper whenever possible. To learn more about the Green Press Initiative, visit www.greenpressinitiative.org.*

Library of Congress Cataloging-in-Publication Data
A catalog record for this book is available from the Library of Congress.

P	21	20	19	18	17	16	15	14	13	12	11	10	9	8	7	6	5	4	3	2	1
Y	32	31	30	29	28	27	26	25	24	23	22	21	20	19	18	17	16	15	14		

Contents

Preface

EPISTEMOLOGY IS A BRANCH OF PHILOSOPHY that deals with the nature of our knowledge. And while it is something that philosophers normally deal with, it holds major importance for all aspects of human life. When scientists, for example, make a discovery, they employ a particular epistemological method that helps them make discoveries. When theologians formulate doctrinal statements, they do so by relying on a particular source of information. Likewise, when prosecutors argue the guilt of someone who committed a particular crime, they rely on certain kinds of evidence and make a certain kind of inference. All of these disciplines, and many more, make epistemological assumptions. But this is not all. Even apart from these disciplines, normal people do the same thing on a daily basis. When we develop a belief by listening to a person's testimony, seeing something with our eyes or recognizing that two statements are contradictory, we are operating on certain important epistemological assumptions. In the end, we all take epistemological positions on things, even if we do not realize it. Therefore, this branch of philosophy requires proper attention.

This book is an introduction to epistemology that is written from a Christian perspective. It began several years ago with a conversation between its authors about the difficulty our students have with this particular branch of philosophy. There are, of course, good introductions to epistemology, and we find them helpful for various purposes. Yet, many of these volumes are too technical or too focused on a specific topic for beginning philosophy students. Therefore, we have tried to write an introduction that covers the major issues in epistemology while also making the discussion as accessible as possible. We hope that students will find it beneficial.

Many people have helped us think through these issues. We would like to thank our friends and colleagues for their constant encouragement and stimulation on these matters. We especially thank Bruce Little, Greg Welty, Jeremy Evans, Rich Holland, Gary Habermas, Dave Beck, Dave Baggett, Thom Provenzola, Mike Jones, Ed Martin and Craig Hinkson for many helpful conversations on these issues. Likewise, the two blind reviewers of this volume offered comments that helped us sharpen the focus of the book, and we wish to thank them for their time and attention to our work. We would also like to thank Tara Dew, Wesley Davey, Carrie Pickelsimer and Billie Goodenough for their gracious help in editing the manuscript of this book. They have given countless hours to reading and rereading the manuscript in preparation for printing, and we are most grateful for them. Finally, we would like to thank David Congdon and the entire editorial board at InterVarsity Press for encouragement and support on this project. This book would not be possible without the help of these individuals. May God continue to bless each one of them for years to come!

James K. Dew Jr.
Mark W. Foreman
June 28, 2013

1

What Is Epistemology?

HOW DO WE KNOW WHAT WE KNOW? This is the basic question that undergirds the discipline of epistemology. We take it for granted that we know many different things, but we rarely ask this basic question about our knowledge. In fact, most people assume that intellectual questions like these are unimportant and have a great aversion to pursuing them. Yet, because we make errors in judgment that are often costly to us, this is the kind of question that we should take seriously. This is especially true regarding the big choices in life.

This book recognizes the importance of asking these kinds of questions and offers an introductory treatment of the basic questions and issues in epistemology. It is designed for those who have no background in philosophy and lack familiarity with these issues. In this chapter, we deal with preliminary issues and make a case for the importance of epistemology. In the remainder of the book, we offer a brief sketch of the major epistemological issues.

WHAT IS EPISTEMOLOGY, AND WHY DO WE NEED IT?

Philosophy is a discipline that addresses a range of important intellectual questions. For example, some philosophers pursue a branch of philosophy called metaphysics which examines ultimate reality by considering things like the nature of time, freedom, essences, God and the soul, to name just a few. Ethics is a discipline of philosophy that examines morality and human actions. Here, philosophers debate people's actions and moral systems. In contrast to these areas of philosophy, epistemology is a branch of philosophy that deals with the nature and sources of knowledge and develops a theory of knowledge. As such, epistemology is referred to as the study of knowledge. Within this field, philosophers might ask the following kinds of questions:

- What does it mean to say that we know something?
- How do we come to know various things?
- What is truth, and how do we find it?
- What does it mean to have epistemic justification, and is this necessary?
- What are epistemological virtues, and are they helpful for us?
- How reliable are our perceptions?
- Can we have certainty?

These, along with other important questions, represent the kind of things we will look at in this book. We will say a bit more about these questions shortly.

Before we do that, however, we should consider why epistemology is important and why we should give it any attention. For some people, it seems foolish or even arrogant to ask epistemological questions. There is a sense in which this is understandable. After all, most people go through life gaining knowledge about all kinds of things without exploring these kinds of questions. Perhaps, they say, asking epistemic questions is a waste of time and mental energy. And, they might say, philosophers who raise such questions solve no puzzles and only create more intellectual problems.

To these concerns, we offer two kinds of response. First, it is unnatural and unfruitful to avoid epistemological questions. That is, we by our nature as human beings long for knowledge and depend on it for all aspects of life, such that not asking these kinds of questions cuts off natural and needed intellectual growth. Consider, for example, the way a child seeks after knowledge. Children have an unquenchable thirst for understanding about their world. I (Dew) happen to have, by God's good favor, four beautiful children. Watching them grow up is fascinating. They learn to eat, crawl, walk, ride bikes, and much more. But most fun of all, they learn how to think. And when this begins to happen, our conversations explode with questions. As a father, I am daily bombarded with questions about trivial things like the following:

"Daddy, what is a tree?"

"Daddy, why is the sky blue?"

"Daddy, why do we wear shoes?"

"Daddy, do I need to wear clothes today?"

"Daddy, where are you going?"

"Daddy, how do I turn on the Wii?"

"Daddy, why can't we play outside in the night time?"

But trivial questions are not the only kind of questions that my children ask. They also ask about the big things in life. Just when I am not expecting something heavy from them, they might also ask:

"Daddy, what happened to Gramps when he died?"

"Daddy, why do we have to die?"

"Daddy, will my friend who is sick ever get better?"

"Daddy, where does God live?"

"Daddy, when will Jesus come back?"

When children ask such questions, they are trying to understand their world. They come into this world knowing and understanding very little and spend the rest of their lives trying to figure out everything. Seeking knowledge and trying to understand how we get this knowledge is a natural thing for us to do. In fact, sometimes it is hard not to ask epistemological questions.

Also consider the way the world changed by asking epistemological questions. In the seventeenth century, Francis Bacon introduced a new method of gaining knowledge—the inductive method. It is safe to say that advances were already taking place before him, but with Bacon, modern science was thrust forward with a new method capable of discovery and invention. Within a short time, modern science was surging forward, and the world would be forever changed. Today, we reap the benefits of the scientific revolution, which was built on a major epistemological shift. If intellectuals had not been asking these questions then, you would be walking to work instead of driving your car.

We are also reminded of how natural and fruitful it is to seek after knowledge when we consider our lives and careers. Many of us work in jobs that require specific kinds of knowledge or a particular set of skills. If we lacked these, we would not be able to do what we do. Thus, people go to college and trade schools to learn what they need to know. Failure to pursue these kinds of knowledge would greatly limit our ability to work and provide for our families.

As a second way of response, we should note that, for some questions, the stakes are so high that we would be fools not to seek the best possible answers and information that may be available. For example, consider once again the questions that my children often ask me. "Daddy, what happens when we die?" As a Christian, I answer that question in a particular way. I explain to my children how God made us and what happens at death. This response, however, assumes that God does exist and that Christianity is ultimately true. But this raises the question as to how we know that these beliefs are true. When someone loses a loved one, that person, whether a Christian or a non-Christian, naturally wonders whether or not God really exists. And given humanity's general desire to live and avoid death, it is foolish not to seek answers to these philosophical questions. If God does not exist, then one is free to live any way one sees fit. But if God does exist, then how one lives would surely matter a great deal. Thus, the reality of death forces us to think about the existence of God, which in turn forces us to think about how we might know if God exists or not.

Or, consider the way that the legal system works. In the United States, for example, people are often sentenced to death after being convicted of murder. How do we know they committed murder? It might be the case that eyewitnesses saw this particular murder take place and gave a report to the police. Or, it might be the case that there was sufficient circumstantial evidence to warrant a murder conviction. In either case, decisions about life and death are being based on the strength of a particular kind of information. But is it possible that eyewitness testimony is not completely accurate? Perhaps the witnesses thought they saw something that they did not see. And even though there may be sufficient circumstantial evidence to convict someone of murder, it might still be possible that all of this evidence is coincidental and thus the convicted party is innocent. We raise these points not because we are trying to undercut the legal system. Rather, we raise these points to illustrate the way life-and-death decisions are based on epistemological assumptions. We often assume that eyewitnesses see everything as it actually is or that circumstantial evidence is completely conclusive. But these assumptions are possibly false. Failure to engage in epistemological considerations could have dire consequences. Therefore, we suggest that epistemology is an important pursuit for all people, not just for intellectuals and philosophers.

WHO IS THIS BOOK FOR?

There are a large number of excellent books on epistemology. Students who want to pursue epistemology further will have plenty of resources at their disposal to satisfy their curiosity. Yet, over the years we have noticed that those who are new to philosophy have an especially difficult time with epistemology. Philosophy itself is hard enough, but for most students, epistemology is often the hardest of all.

This book is written for those with no background in philosophy. It is easy to find good resources that deal with the information in a more technical or academic fashion or that give greater attention to a particular issue than we have here. Many of these books, however, are too technical for beginning philosophy students. Moreover, books that are accessible for beginning students are often focused on specific topics within epistemology and are not intended to offer a broad introduction. We attempt to survey the major issues in epistemology in a concise and accessible fashion, giving students the basics of what they need to know to go further in philosophy or for pursuing their own unique discipline. In short, this is an epistemology for beginners, not for advanced philosophers.

There is one other important feature of this book—it brings a Christian perspective to bear on the questions of knowledge. This does not mean that our only goal is to tell readers about Christianity. Rather, it identifies our perspective. In most places, our treatment of an issue will be similar to other, non-Christian perspectives. But in other places, we will try to show how certain epistemological issues intersect with a Christian perspective and what Christianity has to say about these issues. A case in point is chapter 9, where we deal with the issue of divine revelation. On this note, let us say something about the kinds of issues we cover in this book.

What Issues Will We Cover?

After the general introduction offered here in chapter 1, chapter 2 examines the question of knowledge. Specifically, it answers the question, What is knowledge? For most students, this is an odd question, but it is significant nonetheless. Chapter 2 traces the history of the answer to this question. This historical treatment goes back to Plato and shows that most philosophers have understood knowledge to be justified true belief. To know something, one must first believe it and have justification for it, and it must in fact be true. Although this definition of knowledge has endured for more than two thousand years, it received a significant challenge in the twentieth century from Edmund Gettier. Chapter 2 outlines what the Gettier problem is and how various philosophers have responded to it.

Chapter 3 focuses on the sources of our knowledge. Specifically, it answers the following question: Where does knowledge come from? To answer this question, the chapter looks at various sources. First, it considers the place of reason in our knowledge. Here we consider the works of Plato and Descartes, who were suspicious of our senses and confident in our ability to use reason. It then looks at other philosophers like Lucretius, Bacon, Locke and Hume, who took a different perspective from that of Plato and Descartes. These empiricists thought that experience played a central role in giving us knowledge. In fact, many of these philosophers thought that knowledge could come only from the senses, experience and observations. This chapter also examines the value of testimony from other people and how this informs our beliefs and provides knowledge. Then, it notes the possibility that we have divine revelation from God and how this might give us knowledge of nonphysical things. Here we do not make a case for revelation, because we do that in chapter 9. Instead, we note the two possible kinds of revelation that we might have—natural and special. Finally, chapter 3 considers faith as a source of revelation, arguing that despite what is often argued by some believers, faith is not a source of information.

Chapter 4 explores the question of truth, answering the questions, What is truth, and how do we find it? Against relativism, it first argues that there are in fact some things that are true of reality. But once this is done, it considers the nature of truth itself. What is it about a particular proposition that allows us to deem it as a true statement? In light of this question, chapter 4 considers various definitions of truth: the correspondence theory of truth, coherentism and pragmatism. According to the correspondence theory, a true proposition will be one that corresponds to the way things really are in the world. If the statement does not correspond, it is not true. As we point out there, this approach has been the dominant view for well over two thousand years. More recently, some philosophers have rejected this view in favor of either coherentism or pragmatism. Coherentists argue that a true statement is one that is consistent with, or coheres with, everything else we believe or think we know. Pragmatism, by contrast, says that true statements are those that work—or are valuable—for a particular individual or group of people. Chapter 4 examines each of these positions, arguing that both coherentism and pragmatism offer some helpful insights in identifying truth claims. After all, if a statement is really true, it will be consistent with other things we know and will work for us. Yet, these two criteria by themselves are insufficient as definitions for truth, because a proposition can be consistent with other beliefs and beneficial in some way but still be false. In this chapter we explain how these are necessary conditions for truth but not sufficient conditions for truth. In the end, we argue that a correspondence theory of truth must be affirmed.

In chapter 5 we consider inferences and how they function in our thinking. We first examine the nature of inferences to show how they work and how often we employ them in our thinking, even if we are not consciously aware of doing so. Specifically, we explore the relationship between knowledge claims and the evidence that supports those claims to show how inferences make the interpretive move from evidence to claim. Once this is done, we then describe the different kinds of inferences that we make. Deductive inferences, for example, move from a set of premises to the conclusion. If the premises of a deductive argument are true and the structure of the argument is valid, then the conclusions of these arguments are absolutely certain. Inductive inferences move from a very broad evidential base to make general interpretive claims about that evidence. Unlike deductive inference, induction allows for a vast expansion of knowledge but does not yield absolute certainty. Finally, abductive inference takes one or two pieces of evidence and seeks the best possible explanation of this evidence. This chapter concludes by noting the various errors that we can make in drawing inferences.

Chapter 6 explores the issue of perception. Specifically, it tries to answer the question, What do we perceive? This might seem like an odd question, but it is important. When we see the dog Buddy in front of us, do we see Buddy himself or just some visual representation of him? And, if it is just a visual representation of Buddy, how do we know that our perception of him reflects the way he really is? In light of these kinds of questions, we consider various models of perception. Direct realism, for example, suggests that we see the objects themselves (Buddy) directly and thus we see things the way they really are. But various philosophers have rejected this due to particular problems that it faces. Others have argued for an indirect realism (or representationalism), which says we do not see the objects themselves (Buddy), but rather we see some mental representation of the objects. Indirect realists argue, however, that these representations genuinely reflect the objects themselves. But this view also has some problems. Finally, some have argued for a phenomenological view of perception, which says that we have only mental representations and that these may or may not reflect reality itself. After considering each perspective, we, along with a growing number of philosophers, argue for a return to some form of direct realism. Yet, it is a chastened form of direct realism which recognizes the very real possibility of misperception.

In chapter 7, we address the issue of epistemic justification. In particular, we deal with the question: Do we need justification? We first describe what it means to have epistemic justification and then survey the debate between internalists and externalists about whether or not we need justification. Justification, we note, has to do with being rational about our beliefs. An internalist believes that, in order to be rational, one must have evidence for one's beliefs. In other words, if a person believes that God exists, then she must have reasons for thinking this way if she is to be rational. This is called internalism because it says that a person must have epistemic access to the reasons—she must possess them internally. Externalists disagree, suggesting that for a person to be rational it may not be necessary for him to have reasons and evidence that support his beliefs. After all, they contend, all of us believe various kinds of things without examining the evidential basis for them. After considering this debate between internalists and externalists, we conclude that both have some positives.

Chapter 8 surveys an important issue in epistemology—intellectual virtue and virtue epistemology. We describe what a virtue is, noting that it is some quality or characteristic that produces well-being. By contrast, vices are those qualities or characteristics that are detrimental to the person. While virtue is normally considered to be a moral issue, epistemologists also have a long practice of incorporating virtues into their epistemology. In this chapter, we explain how certain intellectual qualities like studiousness, humility, honesty, courage and carefulness aid and assist us in properly apprehending the world in which we live. In other words, these intellectual qualities help us to see clearly and avoid epistemological error.

In chapter 9, we address an issue that is unique to our introduction to epistemology—divine revelation. Specifically, we consider whether or not there is such a thing as divine revelation. We argue that we are within our epistemic rights for believing that God has revealed himself to us. In fact, we argue that this revelation comes in two basic forms—general and special. As Christian theologians have long argued, natural revelation is the revelation that God has given us of himself, which is found in the created order. We consider the various kinds of theological, scientific and philosophical objections to natural revelation that have been given but argue that these arguments are not convincing. We conclude that this revelation is limited in what it can tell us about God and nonphysical things, but it is there nonetheless. Special revelation is the revelation that God has given us about himself that comes to us through Jesus Christ and the Bible. In this chapter, we are especially interested in our rationale for believing that Jesus and the Bible give us information about God. In short, our approach is christocentric. We argue that because of the resurrection of Jesus, we have good reason to think that he was who he claimed to be. If that is the case, then he gives us information about God, and so does the Bible.

Chapter 10 concludes the book by exploring the problem of skepticism and the possibility of having certainty. Skepticism offers a grim outlook about the possibilities of knowledge. We first survey the different kinds of skepticism, such as methodological skepticism, metaphysical skepticism and Pyrrhonian skepticism. After this, we look at the leading skeptical thinkers throughout history to see why they said what they did. Here we look at Pyrrho of Ellis, Sextus Empiricus, René Descartes, David Hume and Immanuel Kant. After considering the different reasons that skeptics have given, we argue that they offer good reminders that epistemic error is always possible, but they do not justify their ultimate conclusions. There are good reasons for thinking that we can have knowledge. Here we consider these reasons but point out that this still does not yield certainty for the vast majority of our beliefs.

CONCLUSION

Each of these issues will be dealt with in more detail in the following chapters. Students may choose to read this book straight through from beginning to end or may decide to read one particular chapter at a time depending on their interest or need. The book is designed so that either one of these approaches will work.

DISCUSSION QUESTIONS

1. What kinds of issues does epistemology deal with?

2. Despite the suspicions of some, why is epistemology such an important discipline?

2

What Is Knowledge?

WHAT IS KNOWLEDGE? What does it mean to say that you know something? At first, these seem like ridiculous questions. People might not put a lot of thought into what exactly knowledge is even though we *have* knowledge about so many different things. I look outside and say with confidence that the sun is shining and the grass is green. When asked by my children about the first president of the United States of America, I know that it was George Washington. When asked about my family, I know my children's names, birth dates, favorite colors, bad habits and medical history. I know that as I write this paragraph, I am sitting in a hotel lobby in Atlanta, Georgia. Thus, in light of all that we know, we must have some understanding of what knowledge is.

In spite of our general sense of what it means to know, however, the initial questions remain. Even if we have knowledge about many different things, we still have not defined what knowledge is. One might say that knowledge is the intellectual content of our minds. But this description sounds more like a description of ideas. In fact, John Locke and David Hume both define ideas along these very lines. Perhaps knowledge is the same thing as belief. As we will see in a moment, there is clearly a relationship between knowledge and belief, so maybe one can be reduced into the other. But once again, this definition of knowledge has its weaknesses. Claiming that one has knowledge of something seems to imply one has more certitude than merely saying one believes something. When we claim to have knowledge, we claim to have an understanding of the world that is true. When we believe something, we must recognize that beliefs can be wrong or mistaken. Thus, claiming that we know something seems to suggest something more significant than saying that we believe something. In the end, knowing and believing are not the same thing, even if they are related to each other.

It is important to note that we use the word *know* in a number of different ways. Sometimes we use the term to speak of being acquainted with someone: "I know Bill." This is referred to as knowledge by acquaintance. Sometimes we use the word to describe a skill, such as "I know French" or "I know how to play the trumpet." We call this knowledge as competency. Although much can be said about both of these categories, in this book we are not concerned with these kinds of knowledge. Often when we use the word we are talking about knowledge as a truth claim, such as "I know that John F. Kennedy was president of the United States in 1962." This is called a truth claim because it has truth value, meaning it is either true or false. In this book we are concerned with knowing claims like this. We refer to this as propositional knowledge because it comes or can come in the form of a proposition. What does it mean to know in this sense?

How Is Knowledge Typically Defined?

Fortunately, we can look back through the history of philosophy to help answer this question. Dating from the time of Plato and coming up to the present, philosophers have generally defined knowledge in a particular way. According to the traditional approach, knowledge has been defined as possessing three distinct parts or criteria: justification, truth and belief.

Though numerous philosophers could be cited who define knowledge in this way, perhaps the best philosopher to consider is Plato. In *Theaetetus*, Plato presents a dialogue between Theaetetus and Socrates about the nature of knowledge. After rejecting two accounts of knowledge—knowledge as perception only and knowledge as true belief—they define knowledge as something very similar to justified true belief. Socrates says, "Now when a man gets a true judgment about something without an account, his soul is in a state of truth as regards that thing, but he does not know it; for someone who cannot give and take an account of a thing is ignorant about it. But when he has also got an account of it, he is capable of all this and is made perfect in knowledge."[1]

Plato's understanding of knowledge as justified true belief is also in *Meno*. *Meno* is a work famous for the story of the young, uneducated slave who is able to deduce certain geometric truths when properly prompted by Socrates. Plato sets up a dialogue between Socrates and his young friend, Meno, about the nature of virtue. As we read further, we quickly realize that Plato is ultimately arguing for a pre-existent soul within each person. Along the way, however, Socrates and Meno give considerable attention to the issue of virtue. Both agree that a knowledge of virtue is of great importance for virtuous living. They note, however, that it is still possible for people who lack knowledge of virtue to live virtuously as long as they have a "true opinion" about what is the virtuous action in a given case. So then, people can act virtuously because they have knowledge of virtue or because they have the "true opinion" about virtue, even if this true opinion comes about only by coincidence. Now Socrates and Meno affirm that knowledge is better than true opinion, even if both lead to successful decision making. But why? If both produce success, what is the difference between the two, and why should we prefer one over the other?

Plato's answer, via Socrates and Meno, lays the foundation for the traditional definition of knowledge as justified true belief. What is it, they wonder, that distinguishes knowledge from true opinion? Both believe a given proposition, and both affirmations are in fact true. So, if knowledge is better than true opinion, what does knowledge have that true opinion does not? Socrates' answer to the question is simple and straightforward: justification. He says:

> For true opinions, as long as they remain, are a fine thing and all they do is good, but they are not willing to remain long, and they escape from man's mind, so that they are not worth much until one ties them down by giving an account of the reason why. . . . After they are tied down, in the first place they become knowledge, and then they remain in place.[2]

---

[1]Plato, "Theaetetus," in *Plato: Complete Works*, ed. John M. Cooper (Indianapolis: Hackett, 1997), 202c.
[2]Plato, "Meno," in *Plato: Complete Works*, ed. John M. Cooper (Indianapolis: Hackett, 1997), 98a.

For Plato, knowledge is different from true opinion in that knowledge has been tied down by "giving an account of the reason why." In other words, knowledge has some sort of justification, whereas true opinion does not. The person with knowledge enjoys a stronger epistemic position than does someone with true opinion. In the end, Plato's understanding of knowledge includes three criteria: justification, truth and belief. Thus, from Plato forward, knowledge has been defined as justified true belief. Without all three present, an idea or proposition cannot be counted as knowledge. Here is how this works.

Belief. As a first step to knowledge, a person must have a particular belief about something. A belief is something we hold to be true. Take, for example, my claim to know that the earth is spherical. At the most basic level, this claim to knowledge must start as a simple belief. At this point, it is not important why I believe it (that is a matter of justification, which we will get to in a moment). All that is important is that I do in fact believe it. Thus, beliefs seem to be a basic component of knowledge. We cannot know about things that we do not have a belief about. It makes no sense to say, "I know the earth is spherical, but I don't believe it." Yet, it is important to note that believing something does not guarantee that this belief is right. We believe all kinds of things that turn out to be wrong. Compare my belief that the earth is spherical with the view of the ancient philosopher Thales, who believed that the earth was flat. This may have seemed reasonable in ancient times. Yet, as we now know today, this is a false belief. This is one reason why knowledge cannot be identical with belief. Nevertheless, beliefs act as a first step toward knowledge.

Justification. Because beliefs can be wrong, we should want to know if a given belief is true before we can claim to have knowledge of it. This is the matter of justification. In recent years, some philosophers have debated the nature of and need for justification, with some going so far as to say that justification is not essential to having warranted belief. However, throughout most of history philosophers, scientists, theologians and scholars of every other discipline have gone to great lengths to offer justification for their claims to knowledge. The particular mode of justification may differ from person to person or discipline to discipline, but all of them offer some sort of justification for their claims to knowledge. In other words, regardless of their discipline, most people are aware of the fact that they need to offer some rationale for claiming what they claim. Therefore, offering justification for a belief is an important part of the epistemological enterprise. For something to count as knowledge, there must be some justification for the claim being made.

There are at least two considerations to keep in mind when thinking about justification. First, one should understand that justification may come in a variety of different forms, depending on the object under consideration when making a claim to knowledge. We do not know about an apple and God in the same way. We have different sources of knowledge for each (see chap. 3), and thus different forms of justification will be offered. For example, physical objects are of a different nature from nonphysical objects and are supported by different kinds of justification. When making a scientific claim, scientists use tests, observations and experiments to justify their claims. By contrast, theologians generally refer to the Bible[3] or the history of the church when making a case for their claims to knowledge. Likewise, historians, sociologists and philosophers all justify their claims in different ways, depending on what objects they are considering.

Second, one must also realize that the presence of justification is not a guarantee that something is true. Consider, again, Thales' claim that the earth was flat. Why was his view ultimately discarded as wrong? Did his view lack justification? No. His belief may seem naïve, silly or foolish to us today, but when we think about his idea, we can see why he (and others) may have thought this way. For example, when I go to the beach, I look across the horizon at what looks like a flat ocean. Similarly, when I go to the desert, I look across the horizon and see flat land. In short, almost all horizons look flat, giving the impression that the world itself is flat. Without modern science at his disposal, Thales can hardly be blamed for thinking the way that he did. He may have had insufficient justification for his view, but this does not mean that he lacked justification altogether. This reminds us that having justification for an idea does not necessarily mean that an idea or claim is automatically true.

---

[3]We are not suggesting that the theologian cannot use nature (see chap. 10).

Nevertheless, for something to qualify as knowledge, there must be justification for the claim being made.

Truth. So far we have seen that a person can believe things that turn out to be wrong. Knowledge involves much more than simply believing. A person can also hold certain beliefs that enjoy a degree of justification, and still this does not count as knowledge because it is possible for us to have justification for a belief that is still wrong. Therefore, for a claim to count as knowledge, we must have more than just belief and justification. But what else is needed? According to the traditional definition of knowledge, the answer is *truth*. For claims to count as knowledge, a person must have belief and justification, and, in the end, the claim must be true.

Let us consider a concrete example. Suppose that you claim to know that Bill is wearing a blue T-shirt. If you claim to know that Bill's shirt is blue, then you obviously believe that Bill has on a blue T-shirt. So, the belief criterion has been met. Second, in order to say you know that Bill is wearing a blue T-shirt, you must have some sort of justification for that claim. In this case, your justification is that I just told you that Bill's T-shirt is blue, and you have no reason to doubt my word. You now have satisfied the criteria of belief and justification. But it is possible that I am lying or am mistaken about the color of Bill's T-shirt, and in fact he is wearing a gray T-shirt. So, you cannot claim to know that this is true. Rather, for you to have knowledge, it must be the case that Bill's T-shirt is blue. Unless all three criteria are present, then we do not have knowledge.

This definition of knowledge has been firmly established from the time of Plato and was virtually unquestioned throughout most of philosophical history. In more recent times, however, questions about the adequacy of this definition have begun to surface. We now turn to consider some of these questions and how they affect our definition of knowledge as justified true belief (JTB).

What Is Wrong with JTB?

One concern with JTB comes with the distinction made by philosophers between the criteria of justification and truth. Consider once more what is required by JTB. In this account, a person has knowledge if and only if she has belief, justification for that belief, and that belief is in fact true. It is also important to remember that a person can be justified in a belief even if the belief is wrong. But if that is the case, how do we know that the belief is true? In other words, how do we get beyond thinking that our belief is justified to saying that it is true? Consider again my claim to know that the earth is spherical. Why do I think that this is true? In short, I believe it is true because the evidence is overwhelming for this belief. But this evidence, no matter how much of it I might have, is also my justification. Thus, it looks like our beliefs are justified when there is *some* evidence for that belief, and it is counted as true when there is *an overwhelming amount* of evidence for the claim. If so, then the difference between the criteria of justification and truth is a bit vague.

The most significant challenge to the traditional definition of knowledge, however, came in 1963, when a virtually unknown philosopher from Wayne State University named Edmund L. Gettier published a three-page article, "Is Justified True Belief Knowledge?" Gettier quickly outlined the traditional definition and then set forward two cases in which all three criteria are met but knowledge does not result. To get a grasp on what he argued, let us consider his first example. He says:

> Suppose that Smith and Jones have applied for a certain job. And suppose that Smith has strong evidence for the following conjunctive proposition:
>
> (d) Jones is the man who will get the job, and Jones has ten coins in his pocket.
>
> Smith's evidence for (d) might be that the president of the company assured him that Jones would in the end be selected, and that he, Smith, had counted the coins in Jones's pocket ten minutes ago. Proposition (d) entails:
>
> (e) The man who will get the job has ten coins in his pocket.
>
> Let us suppose that Smith sees the entailment from (d) to (e), and accepts (e) on the grounds of (d), for which he has strong evidence. In this case, Smith is clearly justified in believing that (e) is true.
>
> But imagine, further, that unknown to Smith, he himself, not Jones will get the job. And, also, unknown to Smith, he himself has ten coins in his pocket. Proposition (e) is then true, though proposition (d), from which Smith inferred (e), is false. In our example, then, all of the following are true: (i) (e) is true, (ii) Smith believes that (e) is true, and (iii) Smith is

justified in believing that (e) is true. But it is equally clear that Smith does not *know* that (e) is true; for (e) is true in virtue of the number of coins in Smith's pocket, while Smith does not know how many coins are in Smith's pocket, and bases his belief in (e) on a count of coins in Jones's pocket, who he falsely believes to be the man who will get the job.[4]

Despite first appearances, the point being made here is rather simple, even if one has trouble following the technical nature of Gettier's argument. In his final analysis, Gettier contends that the traditional definition of knowledge as justified true belief "does not state a sufficient condition for someone's knowing a given proposition."[5]

A brief explanation of what it means to have a sufficient condition will be helpful here. A sufficient condition is often contrasted with a necessary condition. Simply put, a necessary condition is a condition required for something to be the case but might not itself guarantee that something will be the case. For example, oxygen is necessary for fire, but by itself oxygen is not sufficient to have a fire. By contrast, a sufficient condition is a condition that, if met, will guarantee that something will be the case. For example, if it rains, the street will be wet.

In his examples, Gettier argued that JTB fails as a sufficient condition for knowledge. In other words, as his examples show, one can have belief, justification and truth, but that still does not guarantee one has actual knowledge. It is always possible that the justification being used is faulty or mistaken. Since Gettier's short article, similar examples have been given by other philosophers that are much easier to follow. Two examples will help us better see Gettier's point.

Suppose a friend asks you what time it is. You look at the clock and see that it says 2:10, and you then reply to your friend that it is 2:10. As it turns out, at the moment you say that it is 2:10, it actually *is* 2:10. In this case, all three components of knowledge are present: You believe it is 2:10, you have justification for saying that it is 2:10 (the clock on the wall), and in fact it *is* 2:10. Now, about twenty or thirty minutes later, your friend asks again what time it is. When you look at the wall, you notice that the clock still says 2:10. You are not sure how much time has

[4]Edmund L. Gettier, "Is Justified True Belief Knowledge?", *Analysis* 23, no. 6 (June 1963): 122.
[5]Ibid., 123.

gone by, but you know that at least twenty or thirty minutes have passed since you last looked at the clock. You quickly realize that the batteries in the clock on the wall are dead and that the clock is not really telling time. Evidently, it was just a coincidence that it actually was 2:10 when you first looked at the clock on the wall. When you first said that it was 2:10, did you have knowledge? Gettier would say no because your justification was invalid. The reason you felt justified in saying that it was 2:10 was that the clock said so. But if the batteries in the clock are dead, then the justification is invalid, because it was a coincidence that it was 2:10 when you first looked at the clock. You had a justified true belief, but, according to Gettier, this does not count as knowledge because the justification is faulty.

One more example will make this even clearer. Suppose you walk into the room and find an author standing to the side of the room with a broad smile on his face. He is actually in the room. From this, you quickly form a belief that he is in the room, and then you claim to know he is in the room. Because the author actually is in the room, you have JTB. You believe he is there, you see him (which gives you justification), and it is actually true that he is in the room. Now suppose that the figure you saw to the side of the room is not actually the author but is a life-size cardboard cutout of him which originally caused you to believe you saw him. But if he really is in the room, then where is he? As it turns out, he is on the other side of the room with his back to you; he is wearing a funny wig, such that you never would have recognized him unless someone pointed him out. Once again, you believe he is in the room, you have justification that he is in the room, and he actually is in the room. You have JTB, but this has not been a sufficient condition for you to claim you actually have knowledge. In both examples we have looked at here, it is a matter of coincidence that you affirmed a true statement.

Prior to Gettier's article in 1963, many philosophers unhesitatingly affirmed JTB as an adequate definition of knowledge. Since then, however, philosophers have been much less confident. It seems that Gettier-type examples present a genuine problem for JTB. In particular, the Gettier problem reminds us that it is possible that our justification, even when we have it, may be faulty or founded on weak or invalid inferences.

Therefore, it appears that JTB is not sufficient for knowledge. It may still qualify as a necessary condition, but this is not what adherents of JTB affirmed. JTB might give us a sense of what knowledge is, but it does not give us complete understanding.

Philosophers have responded to Gettier in a number of ways. Some have suggested the need for a fourth criterion for knowledge. In other words, some think that in addition to justification, truth and belief, another condition must be added. One of the more promising options for this is sometimes referred to as the defeasibility condition. In 1969, Keith Lerher and Thomas Paxson wrote an influential article defending the formulation in which they said:

> We propose the following analysis of nonbasic knowledge: S has nonbasic knowledge that h if and only if (i) h is true, (ii) S believes that h, and (iii) there is some statement p that completely justifies S in believing that h and no other statement defeats this justification.[6]

In other words, they think that knowledge might be defined as *undefeated*, justified, true belief. Here, JTB holds up as long as the justification remains valid or undefeated. If, however, the justification for a belief is defeated, then one cannot claim to have knowledge. At first blush, this addition to JTB seems to be very promising. After all, if our justification for our claims is right and the claim is actually true, then it looks like knowledge does in fact follow. Yet, it seems hard to know if we can rule out the possibility of defeaters for every justification that we have. There are some things we are justified in believing that we do not currently have any defeaters for. But this does not mean, however, that no such defeaters exist. Therefore, we might wonder how we know that there are in fact no actual defeaters for everything we claim to know. Even with Lerher and Paxson's defeasibility condition added to JTB, it looks like we will still have this question. But then maybe we do not need certainty in order to have knowledge (an issue we will address in further chapters).

Other philosophers have responded to Gettier, not by adding to JTB

---

[6]Keith Lerher and Thomas Paxson Jr., "Knowledge: Undefeated Justified True Belief," *The Journal of Philosophy* 66, no. 8 (1969): 227.

but by making some alterations to it. For example, in a reliabilist account of knowledge, someone has knowledge of something if she believes it is true, it is in fact true, and her belief of its truthfulness was formed under reliable belief-forming processes. This appears to offer a better definition of knowledge than JTB, because in the JTB model, there is no guarantee that the justification is legitimate. Yet, even here, one may rightly wonder how it is that she can know her belief was formed in a reliable way.[7] This approach may do better than the traditional JTB approach, but even this is not foolproof.

In the end, philosophers are still trying to figure out the best way to resolve the Gettier problem. It should be noted, however, that the Gettier problem does not destroy JTB as an understanding of knowledge. As pointed out earlier, JTB does seem to give us a sense of what knowledge is and can still be thought of as a necessary condition for knowledge. At best, it shows that JTB is not a sufficient condition for knowledge because a person with JTB has no guarantee of knowledge. As the Gettier examples show, there are some cases where JTB seems to fail. But it should be noted that these are rather odd and unusual instances that most of us do not face on a day-to-day basis. In the vast majority of cases, a person with JTB seems to have legitimate claims to knowledge. Furthermore, as the Gettier problem illustrates, the weakness of JTB revolves primarily around the issue of justification. In all cases, the person has justification for the belief, but the justification turns out to be illegitimate. This possibility should not cause despair or skepticism. Instead, it underscores the need for caution and critical evaluation in dealing with the issue of justification. Additionally, it reminds us of the difficulty of gaining absolute certainty (an issue for later chapters) in our quest for knowledge. Despite all these things, however, JTB continues to be a helpful way of thinking about knowledge, even if it does not say everything that needs to be said about the nature of knowledge.

---

[7]As will be noted later, reliabilists claim that one does not need to *know* whether the belief was formed through a reliable process as long as *in fact* it was formed by a reliable process. It is like knowing a fact is true and the fact actually being true. One is an epistemological issue (knowing); the other is an ontological issue (being).

CONCLUSION

As we have seen, knowledge has traditionally been defined as justified true belief (JTB). Gettier's examples remind us that it is possible for our justification to be weak or poorly formed, but this does not mean that JTB is of no help to us in thinking about what it means to know something. In the next chapter, we consider the sources of knowledge and how beliefs are formed.

DISCUSSION QUESTIONS

1. How have philosophers traditionally defined knowledge?

2. Who are some of the important philosophers who have defined knowledge as JTB?

3. Who was Edmund Gettier, and what challenge did he present for JTB?

4. How have recent philosophers responded to the Gettier problem?

5. In light of the Gettier problem, is JTB of any value to us as we think about knowledge?

3

Where Does Knowledge Come From?

NOW THAT WE HAVE LOOKED at the traditional definition of knowledge (knowledge as justified true belief, or JTB), it is time to consider the sources of our knowledge. That is, where does knowledge come from, or where do we get it? Is there one source of knowledge or many? If there is more than one source, is there one that is better than all the rest? Given all that we claim to know and the various ways we claim to know, these are the kinds of questions we should think through. Fortunately, there is a long history of dialogue on these issues and much we can learn from the past. This has been a major issue in philosophy since the time of Plato. In the seventeenth and eighteenth centuries it was a major question for philosophers and scientists alike, and it is still significant due to the progress of modern science. Indeed, this is a question of no small importance.

In what follows, we will briefly describe five possible sources of knowledge. Philosophers sometimes offer more than these five, and sometimes they offer fewer. Yet, these five sources represent some of the most common approaches that epistemologists have taken. We will give a brief history of each approach and look at how various philosophers have argued in their favor. Moreover, we will look at their strengths and weaknesses and how the sources work together.

HOW DOES REASON GIVE US KNOWLEDGE?

According to some philosophers, knowledge is gained, or at least best gained, by the use of reason. This approach is often referred to as rationalism and has a long and rich legacy in philosophical literature. Often, very skeptical of the senses and their ability to render accurate information about reality, rationalists rely on the mind and reason to discover and investigate truth. This kind of knowledge is sometimes referred to as *a priori* knowledge because it is knowledge that one can or does have apart from experience of the external world. By way of reflection and analysis of ideas themselves, rationalists try to discover ideas that are reliable or certain. In short, rationalists believe that reason is the best source of knowledge.

Rationalism enjoys a long and robust history in philosophy. In the ancient world, thinkers like Plato and the Stoics stand out as good examples. In modern history, thinkers like Descartes, Leibniz and Spinoza are also part of the story. To help us understand how reason has been used as a source of knowledge, let us consider two examples: Plato and Descartes.

Plato's (429–347 B.C.) use of reason is evident throughout many of his works. As one who believed ultimate reality was metaphysical, as opposed to physical, this is not surprising. In his doctrine of the forms, he argued that ultimate reality was not in the individual physical objects of our experience, which are subject to constant change, but in the metaphysical entities known as forms. The forms, according to Plato, are unchanging abstract metaphysical entities that transcend time and space, are unmixed with any other entities or qualities and are the model for all physical objects that resemble the form itself. These forms—ultimate reality—are reflected in the physical order of our common experience. So, for example, take our experience of beauty. All of us experience many beautiful things in our lives. Yet, as we think about them, their physical properties are often very different. I might see a woman's face and say, "She is beautiful." Or, I might see a sunset and blurt out, "That sunset is beautiful." Many other things could be listed here of which we would ascribe beauty (mountain landscape, river basin, starry sky, red rose). In each case, we realize that the physical properties of the objects are different and distinct. And yet, in all cases, we ascribe beauty to them. This raises a question: If their physical properties are all different, what is it that makes something beautiful? Because the physical qualities of these objects differ and are subject to change, Plato suggested that beauty must have an objective existence of its own beyond the physical changing realm. Thus beauty, as an objective essence or form, exists apart from the physical objects but is reflected in the physical objects of the world. To be clear, Plato was not denying the existence of the physical objects of our perception. Rather, he was suggesting that these are what they are because they resemble the form.

Because the physical objects are subject to change, Plato was hesitant to build a theory of knowledge based on the physical world. Instead, he felt that knowledge should be based on things that are unchanging and fixed. This meant that Plato's theory of knowledge would be based on his doctrine of the forms. But because the forms are not seen or experienced in the physical world, knowledge is not and cannot be based on our experiences. Rather, Plato's theory of knowledge made use of reason and reflection as they considered the forms themselves.

Plato proposed that there were two worlds or realms of existence. The physical realm is the world of becoming in which objects experience continual change. The metaphysical realm is the world of being which is populated by the forms, archetypes of the objects in the physical realm. The philosopher Heraclitus stated that one cannot know that which continually changes. Plato responded that what one actually knows are the forms, which never change. While one perceives the objects in the physical realm with the senses, one perceives the forms through the intellect. As one perceives objects in the physical realm what one actually knows are the forms in the metaphysical realm, and therefore one gains greater certitude and comes to real knowledge. For example, in *Phaedo*, Socrates is preparing for his death and fielding questions from two of his friends about why he is so competent and fearless in his final hours of life. As he makes a case for the soul, the good and heaven, Socrates (the mouthpiece of Plato) also explains how he thinks we gain true knowledge. While speaking about the forms themselves, Socrates asks Simmias:

> Have you ever grasped them with any of your bodily senses? I am speaking of things such as Bigness, Health, Strength and, in a word the reality of other things, that which each of them essentially is. Is what is most true in them contemplated through the body, or is this the position: whoever

of us prepares himself best and most accurately to grasp that thing itself which is investigating will come closest to the knowledge of it?[1]

When Simmias offers his agreement, Socrates goes on to say:

> Then he who will do this most perfectly who approaches the object with thought alone without associating any site with his thought, or dragging in any sense perception with his reasoning, but who, using pure thought alone, tries to track down each reality pure and by itself, freeing himself as far as possible from eyes and ears and, in a word, from the whole body, because the body confuses the soul and does not lower to acquire truth and wisdom whenever it is associated with it.[2]

In the *Republic*, Plato illustrated this with his analogy of the divided line.[3] As he explains, reality itself might be split into two different realms: the physical below, and the metaphysical (see fig. 3.1).

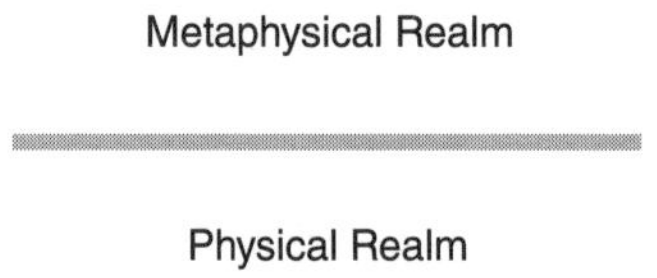

Metaphysical Realm

Physical Realm

Figure 3.1. Plato's Two Realms of Reality

Here the horizontal line represents how reality can be divided into physical and metaphysical realms. Plato then added a vertical line, which illustrated the dominant role that reason plays in his theory of knowledge (see fig. 3.2).

As you see, with reality split into two realms, Plato thought that knowledge was gained only when one considered the forms, and not when one considered the physical world. Of the physical world, one could have only imagination and belief. Thus, for Plato, reason played an enormous role in the acquisition of human knowledge.

René Descartes (1596–1650) is another example of how philosophers have used reason as a source of knowledge. Descartes is often referred to

---

[1]Plato, "Phaedo," in *Plato: Complete Works*, ed. John M. Cooper (Indianapolis: Hackett, 1997), 57.
[2]Ibid.
[3]Plato, "Republic," in *Plato: Complete Works*, ed. John M. Cooper (Indianapolis: Hackett, 1997), 1130-31.

as the father of modern philosophy because of the way he shifted the emphasis of philosophy to the issue of epistemology. For Descartes, two questions were central to his philosophical pursuits: How do we know what we know, and can we have any certainty? Descartes received a world-class education and was exposed to all the great thinkers of history. As he considered all of these thinkers, he was bothered by the disagreement and lack of consensus that he found among them. What he wanted most was a way to establish his knowledge with absolute certainty.

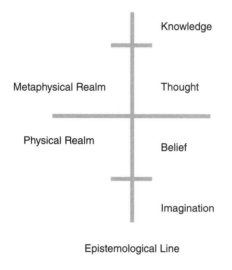

Knowledge

Metaphysical Realm   Thought

Physical Realm   Belief

Imagination

Epistemological Line

Figure 3.2. The Role of Reason in Plato's Theory of Knowledge

However, many people have found Descartes's method to be surprising. Descartes decided that he would doubt everything except for those ideas which were clear and distinct in his mind. So, for example, any idea that might possibly be doubted must be set aside as an improper basis for belief and knowledge. If, however, an idea presented itself with force and un-shakable certainty, Descartes felt it could be used as the basis for the theory of knowledge. With this, Descartes began considering all of the ideas presented to him from his experience. He quickly found that almost every-thing could be doubted. For example, he could doubt the reality of the wall before him, the ground beneath them, the person beside him, and even, he discovered, his own body. But if his own body possibly did not exist, then perhaps he himself did not exist either. At this point, however, Descartes found what he thought to be his first clear and distinct idea: that he himself necessarily existed. Descartes could doubt the existence of his body, but he could not doubt that he himself existed. As he noticed, he was clearly doubting. But if he was doubting, then he must actually be thinking. And, if he was thinking, then he must actually exist to be thinking. This train of thought led to one of the most famous statements in the history of philosophy: "I think, therefore I am." Descartes says:

> Considering the fact that all the same thoughts we have when we are awake can also come to us when we are asleep, without any of them being true, I resolved to pretend that all the things that had ever entered my mind were no more true than the illusions of my dreams. But immediately afterward I noticed that, while I wanted us to think that everything was false, it necessarily had to be the case that I, who was thinking this, was something. And noticing that this truth—I think, therefore I am—was so firm and so assured that all the most extravagant suppositions of the skeptics were incapable of shaking it, I judge that I could accept it without scruple as the first principle of the philosophy I was seeking.[4]

Plato and Descartes both relied on reason and reflection to establish their ideas and make knowledge claims. Plato was suspicious of the senses because they can mislead us and because the physical world is subject to change, so the senses and empirical data were not a reliable guide in the pursuit of knowledge. Instead, he employed reason and reflection in the consideration of the forms and the metaphysical realm for his theory of knowledge. In Descartes's case, he was suspicious of the senses and thought that everything presented to us in our common experience of the physical world could ultimately be a deception. So, like Plato and others who rely on reason, Descartes questioned sense and experience as proper means for gaining knowledge, and he elevated rational reflection.

Before leaving our consideration of reason as a source of knowledge, it is worth saying something about a closely related source of knowledge. Earlier we said that reason is sometimes referred to as *a priori* knowledge because it is knowledge that one can or does have apart from experience

---

[4]René Descartes, *Discourse on Method* (Indianapolis: Hackett, 1998), 18.

of the external world. The same might also be said about intuition or common sense. Many of us claim to know things or affirm things based on what we would call common sense or intuition. These claims are not normally based on our reflections on the world around us but are still *a priori* in the sense that we claim them as true without some kind of justifying experience. But what is an intuition? Intuition is defined as knowledge arrived at immediately. By "immediate" we do not mean quickly; we mean "without a mediator." Most of our knowledge is mediated to us through our senses or reason. Intuition is knowledge that is obtained without employing our senses or reason. If we know something intuitively, then we just know it. According to some philosophers, an intuition might be thought of "as theoretical hunches of a sort: that is, unrefined, relatively spontaneous belief that something is (or is not) the case."[5] In other words, there are some ideas we hold for which we may not necessarily have well-thought-out reasons but nevertheless *seem* to be right. They appear to us as a matter of common sense, and thus we rightly want to maintain these beliefs. Yet, these intuitions might be influenced by certain theoretical ideas or our individual backgrounds and presuppositions. Most philosophers allow intuitions a degree of credence but are cautious about building a theory of knowledge on them.

How Does Experience Give Us Knowledge?

In contrast to those philosophers who developed a theory of knowledge based on reason and reflection, numerous philosophers in the ancient and modern world have taken a much different approach. For empiricists, or any epistemologist who relies on experience and sense data, knowledge is gained through experience and the senses. In particular, these philosophers emphasize the role our perceptions of the physical world play in our knowledge claims. As human beings, we have all kinds of different experiences. For example, we experience things in relationships with other people, we have perceptions about the world around us, and we experience feelings and emotions. But for most empiricists, it is the experiences offered to us from our senses that matter the most.

---

[5]Paul K. Moser, Dwayne H. Mulder and J. D. Trout, *The Theory of Knowledge: A Thematic Introduction* (New York: Oxford University Press, 1998), 111.

There are different kinds of empiricists. Some might be classified as hard empiricists, who claim that knowledge comes *only* from the senses. Others, however, could be classified as soft empiricists, because they merely claim that most knowledge comes to us through the senses. And, to be clear, empiricists do not suggest that reason plays no part in our knowledge. Rather, they affirm that all knowledge is dependent on the senses in some way or the other. It is common to find these thinkers reflecting on what they gain from their senses and subjecting these ideas to rational reflection. Several examples will be helpful for us to understand this approach to knowledge.

In the ancient world, Epicureanism—based on the teachings of Epicurus (341 B.C.–270 B.C.)—is an obvious example of empiricism. In the first century B.C., Epicureanism was popularized by Lucretius (99 B.C.–55 B.C.) in *The Nature of Things*. Like other Epicureans, Lucretius held to a shockingly modern view of the physical world. In the view of the Epicureans, all of reality is physical and composed of tiny particles called atoms. These atoms are eternal, indestructible and unchangeable. Moreover, there are a limited number of kinds of atoms, but there is an infinite number of each kind of atom. Thus, the Epicureans held a radically materialistic view of reality.

This view of reality had enormous implications for both ethics and epistemology. Normally, discussions on Epicureanism arise in relation to ethical or moral issues. In fact, for most people, Epicureanism is known only for its claim that pleasure is the purpose of life. The Epicureans thought this way for a simple reason. If all of reality consists of physical things, then the soul cannot survive death. And, because there is no life after death, then one does not have to worry about judgment, punishment or hell. Therefore, morally speaking, people do not have to worry about being good but only about fulfilling their desires. What is most important for our discussion here, however, is the way that the Epicurean view of reality influenced their theory of knowledge. Because the physical world is all there is to reality, knowledge of any kind must be about the physical world and nothing else. And, because we know the physical world through our senses, knowledge itself is dependent on experience and not reason. When and where the senses give us direct information about the world, Epicureans thought we are obliged to accept it as true.

In modern history, empiricism has played an enormous role in Western epistemology. Modern science, for example, is a major enterprise based on empirical methods and is highly esteemed in modern culture due to its extraordinary success. Though there was plenty of good science happening before his time, much of this began in the seventeenth century with Francis Bacon (1561–1626). In contrast to the Aristotelian approach of deduction, Bacon wrote his *Novum Organum* (*New Method*) to introduce a new scientific method: the inductive method. With the old method of deduction, scientists started with certain general ideas or axioms that were held to be true and then interpreted all of their observations about nature through the lens of the general axiom. The greatest problem Bacon saw with this method was its lack of emphasis on thorough experimentation and observation. In short, he felt that scientists typically moved too quickly past the particular details observed in the physical world in the formulation of their theories. This, according to Bacon, was the reason there had been so little discovery and advancement in science before him. He says, "The sciences are almost stopped in their tracks, and show no developments worthy of the human race. . . . The whole tradition of the disciplines presents us with a series of Masters and pupils, not a succession of discoveries and disciples who make notable improvements to their discoveries."[6]

To counter this, Bacon presented his new method of induction, which emphasized thorough experimentation and observation of the physical world at the heart of the scientific enterprise. Comparing the old method with his new method, Bacon says:

> There are, and can be, only two ways to investigate and discover truth. The one leaps from sense and particulars to the most general axioms, and from these particulars and their settled truth, determines and discovers intermediate axioms; this is the current way. The other elicits axioms from sense and particulars, rising in a gradual and unbroken ascent to arrive at last at the most general axioms; this is the true way, but it has not yet been tried.[7]

---

[6]Francis Bacon, *The New Organum* (New York: Cambridge University Press, 2000), 7.
[7]Ibid., 36.

So, with Bacon there was a new emphasis on empirical data in the natural sciences. From him forward all sciences paid careful attention to the particular details of reality in their observations. When done properly, scientific theories will always be grounded in empirical data.

John Locke (1632–1704) is probably one of the most famous empiricists in the history of philosophy. Locke suggested that ideas are the mental objects of the mind that represent the external world. All ideas, according to Locke, come to us through our senses, and apart from these, we have no other knowledge. Rejecting those who taught that the mind possessed certain innate ideas, Locke suggested that at birth the mind was *tabula rasa*—a blank slate. In other words, we are not born with any natural ideas already present in the mind. Rather, all ideas and knowledge come to us through our senses and experiences. He says, "Let us then suppose the mind to be, as we say, white paper, devoid of all characters, without any ideas; how comes it to be furnished? . . . To this I answer, in one word, from *experience*: in that, all our knowledge is founded; and from that it ultimately derives itself."[8]

Locke also made a clear distinction between two different kinds of ideas: simple ideas and complex ideas. For Locke a simple idea consists of a mental representation of one single quality, unmixed with any others. For example, as I hold my coffee mug in my hand, I perceive many different qualities about the mug: white, hot, ceramic, smell of coffee. According to Locke, each one of these individual qualities should be thought of as a simple idea. Simple ideas are set in contrast by Locke to complex ideas. In the example just given, white and hot serve as examples of simple ideas, but the idea of the mug as a whole represents what Locke classifies as a complex idea. For Locke, complex ideas are built from many different simple ideas presented to the mind. He says, "Ideas thus made up of several simple ones put together, I call complex; such as beauty, gratitude, a man, an Army, the universe."[9]

One of the most famous empiricists was David Hume (1711–1776), who represents a radical form of empiricism. Hume is often referred to

---

[8]John Locke, *An Essay Concerning Human Understanding* (London: Penguin, 2004), 109, emphasis his.
[9]Ibid., 159.

as a skeptic because of the restrictions he placed on what we can claim to know. Hume divided knowledge into two kinds (known as Hume's fork), relations of ideas and matters of fact. Relations of ideas are those propositions that are logically true and therefore certain but tell us nothing about reality. Mathematical ideas like 2 + 2 = 4 and pure definitions like "All triangles have three angles" and "All mothers are women" would fit under this category. The concepts would be true even if nothing existed at all, and we determine they are true by analyzing the meaning of the terms (thus they are often referred to as "analytic"). Matters of fact, by contrast, are impressions of reality based on sense perceptions. The impression in my mind, "I have a blue car," is based on my looking at my car and seeing that it is blue. However, Hume claims we can never be certain of such claims. Why can't we have certainty?

Hume claims that I am locked into knowing only what my senses tell me. I am completely dependent on my senses for my knowledge of the world. But how do I know that what senses tell me about the world really is the case? My senses tell me my car is blue, but how do I know that my sense perception is reliable and that my car really is blue? Hume says the only way I could do that is to be able to get outside of my own mind, to perceive the world apart from my senses and see if they are reliable. But how do I do that when I need my senses to perceive? My wife works in a medical laboratory where they use a number of diagnostic instruments. How do they know the instruments are giving the accurate information? They employ a series of quality control tests to determine the reliability of their instruments. However, there do not seem to be any quality control tests for my senses because I have to use them in order to do the tests. This is called the egocentric predicament. Hume says that all we can claim to know are the phenomena of our own experiences, but we cannot know what reality is with any certainty outside of those experiences. This causes Hume to reject all sorts of metaphysical claims as knowledge including, of course, religious claims. He states:

> When we run over libraries persuaded of these principles what havoc must we make? If we take in our hands any volume of divinity or school metaphysics, for instance, let us ask: Does it contain any abstract reasoning concerning quantity or number? No. Does it contain any experimental

reasoning concerning matter of fact and existence? No. Commit it then to the flames. For it can contain nothing but sophistry and illusion.[10]

There are plenty of others who might be listed here as important examples of empiricists, among them Isaac Newton and George Berkeley. What is important to note at this point, however, is that empiricists emphasize the role of our senses, experiences and observation in the formation of knowledge. This approach was taken by many of the ancients as well as many in the modern period.

Is Testimony of Any Value?

One other important source of knowledge, which has not received much attention until recently, is personal testimony. We interact with other people, listen to their stories and rely on their reports for things that we have not seen for ourselves. For the most part, we do not consider this to be illegitimate or problematic. In fact, we often make important decisions in our lives based on testimonial evidence or considerations. For example, testimony given in a court of law or a police station during interrogation is often held to be powerful and persuasive in most Western legal systems. With regard to our religious belief systems, we also rely heavily on the testimony of others and what they have experienced or seen about God. But these are not the only ways that we rely on testimony. Consider the way we depend on it for normal situations in life. As I stand in front of my closet in the morning trying to figure out what to wear for that day, I might ask my wife or my children if it is raining outside or if it looks particularly cold that day. While waiting at a stop sign to turn left onto a highway, I might ask the person sitting in the passenger seat if there any cars coming from the right side of the car, which is blocked by some physical object. Or, if I am late for an appointment and want to know who is already present in the meeting, I might call my secretary and ask who has already arrived and who else they are waiting on. In all these cases, we rely on what others tell us about the world when we ourselves do not have access to that information.

---

[10]David Hume, *An Inquiry Concerning Human Understanding*, ed. Charles W. Hendel (Indianapolis: Bobbs-Merrill, 1955), 173.

Generally speaking, we accept the testimony of other people without suspicion or hesitation. And as long as we have no good reasons for rejecting a testimony, it is sensible to accept it. Yet, as epistemologists would point out, one must be careful when relying on this particular source of knowledge. To begin with, personal testimony is not a firsthand source of knowledge like reason or experience. In both of those cases, the person has immediate and direct access to the thoughts of her mind as she considers a given issue, or to the sensations and perceptions presented to her mind by experience. In the case of testimony, however, we do not have immediate and direct access to the information because it comes from another person. This raises the greatest concern with personal testimony as a source of knowledge. Because people sometimes lie, exaggerate or are motivated by selfishness, it is possible that their testimony could be untrue. For example, when politicians report horrible things about their opponents in a political campaign as a scare tactic to get themselves elected, we should probably be suspicious of what they have to say. Furthermore, even in cases where people's motives may be pure and genuine, it could still be possible that they have forgotten important details, are themselves misinformed or are incompetent physically or mentally. My near-deaf grandfather, for instance, might be the most honest person I have ever known. But I should be cautious when he reports details of conversations or speeches given in a noisy room. Likewise, when someone I know is heavily medicated in such a way that she hallucinates or dreams out loud, I might wonder if some of her claims are really true.

But how problematic are these concerns? Do they render all testimony invalid or inadequate as a source of knowledge? What if the testimony we receive comes from people who are trustworthy and competent physically and mentally? Moreover, what if the testimony we receive fits very well with other things we know to be true about a given issue? In these cases, most of us feel that it is rational to accept such testimony because there seems to be no good reason for rejecting their claims. Yet, because of the possible difficulties just mentioned, we still might wonder how we know that a given testimony is trustworthy. One quick side note is worthy of our attention here. We should be clear about what kinds of testimony for which we want assurance. When testimony is given about unimportant or uncontroversial issues, we typically do not struggle or hesitate to accept it. Or, when we hear a report that corresponds to, or is coherent with, something else we know to be true, we normally believe it. In these cases, we hear the report and accept it as true without any worry. By contrast, however, when reports are given that seem contrary to something else we believe or know, are controversial in nature or are about something very important, we might hesitate or suspend judgment for a time.

It is normal to be hesitant about a given testimony in cases like these. Instead of categorically dismissing testimony as a source of knowledge, however, the more prudent approach would be to seek other forms of validation or confirmation about the report if there are reasons to be suspicious of the testimony. This is sometimes referred to as the method of triangulation.[11] In this approach, we accept testimony as one piece of a larger web of sources about a given issue or event. The claims which are supported by a greater number of independent sources are normally held to be more reliable. If, however, the testimony is clearly contradicted by other reliable sources, we normally either reject it or continue to suspend judgment. With this, we are able to validate reports and make wise decisions about testimony.

Do We Have Revelation?

All of the sources considered thus far are important sources of knowledge in general. And they are especially important for our knowledge of the world itself. But what about knowledge of God or metaphysics? For this kind of knowledge, most Christians rely on divine revelation. We will consider the issue most fully in chapter 9, but for now let us consider why such revelation would be important.

As Christians, we make many different claims about our God. Yet, we must acknowledge that the majority of these claims are not based on data drawn from the natural world. Christians affirm that God has given us general revelation, but we also admit that this is quite limited. Regarding

---

[11]J. D. Trout, *Measuring the Intentional World: Realism, Naturalism and Quantitative Methods in the Behavioral Sciences* (New York: Oxford University Press, 1998).

the knowledge of God that can be derived from nature, Thomas Aquinas thought that it is possible to know that God exists but not much of what he is like. In other words, one cannot know by looking at nature that God is triune and omniscient or that salvation is through Christ alone. We formulate these affirmations in response to Scripture. Yet, Aquinas did think that nature pointed to the existence of God. Later philosophers, such as Hume and Kant, were more pessimistic than Aquinas about natural revelation. They suggested that nothing can be known of God from the natural order. While Christians might not be willing to go as far as Hume and Kant on this subject, we must admit that most of our knowledge of God is not derived from nature.

Our trust in the Bible as a source of knowledge rests on the authority and trustworthy nature of Jesus Christ. He affirmed that all of the Old Testament was the Word of God, and the New Testament is written as a record of his life and teachings. We will deal with this issue in chapter 9, but for now we note that the Bible offers vital information about God which is necessary for understanding the divine. We believe that God has revealed himself to us in such a way as to make himself known to us.

Is Faith a Source of Knowledge?

Thus far, we have considered reason, experience, testimony and revelation as sources of knowledge. In each case, we have looked at how they offer knowledge and why they are affirmed as reliable sources. This brings us to the issue of faith and whether or not it too is a source of knowledge. For many religious people, especially Christians, faith is often spoken of as a source of knowledge. For example, when asked how they know that God exists, believers might say, "by faith." Or, when we believers are asked how we know that Jesus is the Son of God, we might respond by saying, "I know by faith." In these cases, believers suggest that our faith in the Lord is the basis for our knowledge of him. Although the motivation and devotion of these believers is commendable, we suggest that this is a misunderstanding of what faith is. When properly understood, faith is not a source of knowledge, because it does not give us any new information or knowledge. Rather, faith is a response to the knowledge or information that we receive about God from divine revelation.

Believers sometimes respond to this by saying our relationship to Christ is based on faith and therefore we know Christ by faith. This is true but fails to recognize that the word *know* can be used in at least two different ways. First, the word *know* might be used in an epistemological sense to refer to the way that we find out about something. Or it might be used in a relational sense. When we say that we know Christ by faith, we are using the word *know* in a relational sense; that is, we come into relationship with Jesus Christ and relate to him by our trust response to him, called faith. It does not mean, however, that we learned about Jesus or found out about him by faith. Knowledge of Christ comes by divine revelation (Rom 10:14-17). Thus, to say we know Christ by faith is not an epistemological statement. Epistemologically speaking, then, one does not know things by faith.

At first this may seem as though we are splitting hairs. But it is an important distinction to make for a number of reasons. First, using faith in an epistemological fashion confuses the term and amounts to equivocation. Second, using faith this way allows anyone to affirm anything by faith. In other words, if Christians can say that they know about God by faith, why cannot people with other beliefs say the same thing? One can say that they know cars have souls by faith, or that crystals possess divine powers. Because of these things we suggest that faith, when properly understood, is a response to knowledge but not a source of it.

Conclusion

In this chapter we have discussed the various sources for our knowledge. We have suggested that reason, experience, testimony and revelation qualify as sources of knowledge. We have also suggested that faith is not a source of knowledge. In the next chapter we will consider the issue of truth. In particular, we will consider whether or not there is such a thing as truth, what it is and how we find it.

Discussion Questions

1. What role does reason play in our knowledge, and what have different philosophers said about this?

2. How much of our knowledge comes from experience?

3. Who were some important empiricists, and what did they have to say?

4. What value do testimony and revelation have in our knowledge?

5. Is faith a source of knowledge? Why or why not?

4

What Is Truth,
and How Do We Find It?

SO FAR WE HAVE CONSIDERED our understanding of what knowledge is and where we get our knowledge. In this chapter, we turn our attention to the question of truth. What is truth, and how do we find it? As beings who long for knowledge, this is a vital question for us. Additionally, today there is a raging debate about whether or not there is such a thing as absolute truth or if truth is relative. Questions like these have bearing on almost all matters of human life. Christians, for example, proclaim a message they believe to be not just rational but also true. If, however, nothing is actually true, then all such beliefs are foolish. Likewise, if nothing is actually true, then modern science is an enormous waste of time and energy. In short, all the beliefs that matter the most to us as human beings assume that something really is true. Questions about truth cannot be avoided or dismissed as unimportant. In what follows, we will explore several important questions about truth: Is anything really true, how should we define truth, and how we can know when something is in fact true?

IS ANYTHING REALLY TRUE?
As human beings, we assume that certain things are true about the world we live in. For example, we believe the things we see really do exist and are the way they seem to us. Unless we assume this, it would be incredibly difficult for human beings to function. Nevertheless, some philosophers and intellectuals contend that no statements or ideas are true. For ex-

ample, postmodern thinkers take an antirealist perspective that holds all truth claims to be subjective. In other words, they think it is impossible for a person to view reality as it actually is. For them, all of our perceptions come to us through the subjective filters of our minds. They suggest that truth claims fail to appreciate the various ways that our ideas and understanding of reality are shaped and influenced by the world in which we live. Because of this, they contend that absolute truth does not exist.

Before we consider what is truth, we must first consider the postmodern rejection of objectivity. Is there any reason to think that the postmodern antirealists are right in saying that all truth claims are naïvely subjective and fully incapable of making truthful comments about the way things really are? This issue will be treated in much greater detail in a later chapter, but a few comments or observations are in order at this point. In short, the idea that nothing is really true or actually true about reality is a gross overstatement that leads to absurdity. It is one thing for us to have limitations in our ability to grasp fully the details and nature of reality. It is quite another thing, however, to say that we cannot make any true statements about reality and that nothing is objectively true. Those who claim that there is no such thing as truth are met with several significant problems.

First, it is commonly noted that this statement is contradictory. To say that nothing is actually true is to make a statement that something is actually true. Those who make this statement obviously believe that *it* is true, and, by doing so, they contradict themselves.

Second, this position is challenged by the nature of reality itself. If something exists, then something must actually be true about that reality. If nothing else, it would be true to say that the world exists, I exist or something exists. And so, if these things really do exist, then something is true of them.

Third, intuitively speaking, each of us has an overwhelming sense that something is actually true of the world we live in. We may debate what propositions are actually true and at times have difficulty identifying them, but the vast majority of human beings throughout history have had an overwhelming conviction that there is such a thing as truth and that we can know it, at least in part.

Fourth, consider the advancements and accomplishments of modern science. In the past few hundred years, we have gone from horse and buggy to rocket ships that send people into outer space and place people on the moon. We have gained the ability to open a person's body and perform organ transplants, developed medicines to cure many forms of cancer and invented devices that allow deaf people to hear. Likewise, we have created technologies that allow us to speak with people around the world in real time. These are all amazing developments that have come to us through the progress of modern science. If it is impossible to know if something is true or false, then one wonders how such advancements are possible. These developments require us to understand the world properly and accurately. Consider flying to the moon. Having never been to the moon, physicists relied heavily on their measurements and calculations of the physical world to map the trajectory of the rocket. Unless their representations were actually true, landing on the moon would have been impossible. And yet, as we are well aware, they have been successful in doing this numerous times. So, given the success of modern science, it looks like it is possible to speak of truth, search for truth and make truth claims. As Benjamin Myers notes, "postmodern thinkers have typically failed to reckon seriously with the explanatory successes of the natural sciences."[1]

So Then, What *Is* Truth?

Now we turn to the most important question of this chapter: What is truth? Before we begin, it is important to make a distinction between definitions for truth and tests for truth. In the section below, we will consider various ways that truth has been defined and argue that two of these definitions are insufficient. In the next section, however, we will look at tests for truth and will argue that each of these has an important role to play. So then, let us consider the distinction between a definition and a test. A definition describes the nature of an object, concept or event. As we try to define truth, we are particularly interested in comprehending its nature. By contrast, a test for something is a means by

---

[1]Benjamin Myers, "Alister E. McGrath's Scientific Theology," in Alister E. McGrath, *The Order of Things* (Oxford: Blackwell, 2006), 11.

which we identify or locate it. When it comes to truth claims, tests are used to see which ones are right and which ones are wrong.

Generally speaking, there are three different definitions given for truth: the correspondence theory of truth, coherentism and pragmatism. Although the correspondence theory of truth has been the dominant position throughout most of history, we will consider coherentism and pragmatism first. According to coherentists, a proposition is true if it coheres with, or is consistent with, everything else that a person believes. In this approach, the metaphor of a web is often used to illustrate how this will work. In a web, for example, there are many points of intersection where one strand crosses over another strand of the web. Given the overlap of these strands, the web itself is strengthened and is able to function. According to coherentists, a person's belief system is similar to this web and is judged on how well the individual beliefs fit with each other and work together. Each point in the web represents a particular belief held by the individual. If a particular idea or claim fits within the larger web of beliefs and is consistent with them, then we could say the belief is true. So then, what is most important for the coherence model of truth is that claims must relate to each other in a consistent and harmonious fashion. As Doug Groothuis summarizes,

> Coherence theories of truth argue that what makes a statement or belief true is its coherence or consistency with one's other beliefs. If my "web of belief" is large and internally consistent—that is, if none of my beliefs contradict each other—my beliefs are true. A belief is false if it fails to cohere with the rest of my beliefs. In other words, truth is simply defined as logical coherence.[2]

As we will see, coherentism offers a helpful although incomplete way of identifying truth claims. As a definition, however, it seems to be woefully inadequate. As Groothuis goes on to say, "The main problem with this view is that a set of beliefs held by fallible human beings may be coherent, but false."[3] Groothuis raises a legitimate concern with the coherentist understanding of truth. We can think of all kinds of stories to

---

[2]Doug Groothuis, "Truth Defined and Defended," in *Reclaiming the Center*, ed. Milliard Erickson, Paul Kjoss Helseth and Justin Taylor (Wheaton, IL: Crossway, 2004), 73.
[3]Ibid.

tell which are consistent with each other but are still objectively false. For example, consider a childhood classic, the Berenstain Bears stories. In these stories, we are told of a bear family that live in an oak tree and have rather humanlike lives. Papa bear goes off to work, Mama bear works in the kitchen, and Sister and Brother bear go off to school and play outside. These bears face problems, learn lessons, make jokes and show love to each other. All things considered, we would have to grant that the stories themselves are consistent with each other internally. In any given episode or book of the series, we encounter a story that is well crafted and internally consistent with itself.

Plenty of other examples like this could be cited. Consider most fiction movies or novels. When I (Dew) was a child, I was a huge Superman fan. When one of these movies came on television, I dressed up in my Superman pajamas and sat with my eyes glued to the set, soaking in every detail of my great superhero. Even now when these movies come on television, I find myself reliving the joy of my childhood memories. And now that I consider the story itself, it seems to be told in a consistent and coherent fashion. Or, consider a more modern example: the Bourne trilogy, in which Jason Bourne fights to regain his personal identity while struggling against the Central Intelligence Agency, which is trying to eliminate his existence. The story is told in such a way that it does not contradict itself and is consistent.

Yet, in the case of the Berenstain Bears, Superman, Jason Bourne, and almost any other type of fiction, there is a glaring problem: it is fiction, and therefore not actually true. No matter how consistent and coherent the stories might be, the fact is, little bears do not live in trees and speak English, men do not fly around in red capes and lift falling helicopters from the sky, and Jason Bourne is a mere creation of Robert Ludlum for the sake of entertainment. None of these fictional characters are real. Therefore, it looks like coherentism is an insufficient way of defining truth, because it is possible for stories and beliefs to be consistent while being objectively false.

Other contemporary postmodern epistemologists have taken a pragmatic view of truth. At the risk of being overly general, we might say that pragmatism defines truth as a set of beliefs that works for a particular person or group in dealing with reality or accomplishing particular tasks. So then, if a belief helps a person cope with hardship or reach a particular goal, then that belief is counted as true. As Stewart Kelly puts it, "The ballpark idea is that truth is to be construed instrumentally, such that beliefs always prove useful or expedient to those who believe them."[4] There are many different pragmatists we could look at here, such as Charles Sanders Peirce, John Dewey or Richard Rorty. But none captures the spirit of pragmatism better than the American philosopher William James (1842–1910). James pinpoints the pragmatic view of truth when he says, "The truth of an idea is not a stagnant property inherent in it. Truth *happens* to an idea. It *becomes* true, is made true by events."[5] Or put a different way, "The truth is the name of whatever proves itself to be good in the way of belief, and good, too, for definite assignable reasons."[6] He argues that "the whole function of philosophy ought to be to find out what definite difference it will make to you and me, at definite instances of our life, if this world-formula or that world-formula be the true one."[7] So, in short, for pragmatists truth is what works.

As with the coherentist perspective on truth, pragmatism can be helpful in identifying or testing for truth claims, and this benefit will be considered shortly. Yet, like coherentism, pragmatism seems problematic as a definition for truth. Just because a particular idea or belief may work for a person, or bring about a particular outcome, does not mean that the idea or belief is true. As Paul Horwich has noted, "True beliefs tend to foster success. But it happens regularly that actions based on true beliefs lead to disaster, while false assumptions, by pure chance, produce beneficial results."[8] In other words, sometimes true beliefs lead us to act in ways that bring about chaos and heartache. At other times, false beliefs may help us cope with undesirable situations. For example, imagine a little boy named Peter who is dreadfully afraid of the dark and creates

---

[4]Stewart E. Kelly, *Truth Considered and Applied: Examining Postmodernism, History and Christian Faith* (Nashville: B&H Academic, 2011), 283-84.

[5]William James, *Pragmatism* (Amherst, NY: Prometheus, 1991), 89.

[6]Ibid., 36.

[7]Ibid., 25.

[8]Paul Horwich, "Theories of Truth," in *A Companion to Metaphysics*, ed. Jaegwon Kim and Ernest Sosa (Oxford: Blackwell, 1995), 493.

an imaginary big brother who sleeps in his room and keeps the monsters away. Even though this imaginary brother is fictional, the belief in the brother helps Peter deal with his fear of darkness. Here we have identified a fictional belief that is helpful for a particular person. But because this particular belief works for Peter, it should, according to pragmatist criteria for truth, be considered true. Despite the utility of this belief, however, Peter's belief in an imaginary brother is clearly false. And so, just because the belief is helpful or useful to a person does not mean that the belief is true.

But this is not the only problem with a pragmatic view of truth. It seems as though this view would also lead to relativism and be implausible. Consider the example of Peter, who creates an imaginary brother to help him with his fear of darkness. In this case, Peter's belief is helpful for him and thus, according to pragmatists, is true for him. Now consider a different child, Alexa, who creates an imaginary big sister to fight off the monsters in her room, in hopes that this will help her deal with her fear of darkness. In the case of Alexa, however, this belief is not helpful, does not take away her fear and would therefore be, according to pragmatists, false. What we find here is that any given belief may work for one person but not for another. Although some postmodern thinkers may be comfortable with this kind of relativism, it is problematic and difficult for most human beings to accept. As Kelly notes, this understanding of truth "makes a shambles of our intuitive understanding of what it is for something to be true."[9]

Additionally, this view would violate the law of noncontradiction. According to this law, it is impossible for something to be true while its exact opposite is also true at the same time. More formally, it states that both A and non-A cannot be true at the same time, in the same place and in the same way. Now, if we take the pragmatic view of truth to its logical conclusion, then we must be willing to affirm such contradictions. Again, Kelly notes, "If we suppose that P is useful for Dave, but not-P is useful for Susan, then P and not-P would be simultaneously true, a serious problem for any viable theory of truth."[10] And so, whatever benefits

---

[9]Kelly, *Truth Considered and Applied*, 284.
[10]Ibid., 283.

pragmatism might hold for testing truth claims, it is an insufficient way of defining what truth is.

This brings us to our consideration of the correspondence theory of truth. In this approach, truth is defined as that which corresponds to reality. In other words, true propositions or statements are required to fit with, or line up with, what we find in the world. The following statement is an example: "Tina is wearing a blue sweater." In a coherentist perspective, the statement would be counted as true if it was consistent with everything else that a person believed. Yet, as we have seen, it seems that there are some significant problems with this definition of truth. In the pragmatic view, this statement would be judged true because it was helpful to a particular person or group. Here again, there seem to be some problems with this perspective. With the correspondence theory of truth, however, statements like "Tina is wearing a blue sweater" are judged by one simple question: Is it the case that Tina is wearing a blue sweater? If, in fact, Tina is currently wearing a blue sweater, then the statement "Tina is wearing a blue sweater" is true. Notice, what makes this statement true is the fact that the statement corresponds to a real state of affairs in the world. If it had not been the case that Tina was wearing a blue sweater, then this statement would be false. So then, in a correspondence view of truth, truth is defined as that which fits with reality itself.

This theory of truth enjoys a very long and dominant legacy in the history of humankind. Even in the ancient world, philosophers like Plato and Aristotle assumed this perspective. While speaking about the nature of true and false beliefs, for example, Plato says, "A false belief will be a matter of believing things that are contrary to those which are."[11] Even more specifically, Aristotle says, while discussing the nature of truth and falsity, "To say of what is that it is not, or of what is not that it is, is false, while to say of what is that it is, and what is not that it is not, is true; so that he says of anything that it is, or that it is not, will say either what is true or what is false; but neither what is nor what is not is said to be or not to be."[12] Additionally, this perspective has been adopted by the vast

---

[11]Plato, "Sophist," in *Plato: Complete Works*, ed. John M. Cooper (Indianapolis: Hackett, 1997), 261.
[12]Aristotle, "Metaphysics," in *The Complete Works of Aristotle*, ed. Jonathan Barnes (Princeton, NJ: Princeton University Press, 1984), 2:1597.

majority of philosophers and thinkers throughout the medieval and modern period and is still the dominant view today.

Unlike the coherentist and pragmatic definitions for truth, the correspondence theory of truth seems to be much less problematic. For most people, the intuitive appeal of this perspective seems so strong and established by common sense that it is absurd to think any differently. As David Clark has noted,

> Since virtually all people, including those who have never studied episte-mology, typically assume something like this notion of truth, it is a *pre-theoretic* intuition regarding truth. . . . This is pretheoretic in that it is not an idea that *results from* complex theory building about the nature of truth but a belief that people *bring* to their theorizing about truth. It is a basic assumption, rooted in experience. It is something people philosophize *with*, not something they philosophize *to*.[13]

In other words, this perspective seems to be foundational and essential to all of our thinking, dialogue and theorizing about the world in which we live. Without it, it seems as though knowledge of any kind would be impossible. Philosopher John Searle seems to agree with this assessment, noting that this is a default position without which we could not think or talk. Calling the correspondence theory of truth a pre-reflective idea, he argues that "any departure from [this] requires a conscious effort in a convincing argument."[14]

This view of truth also enjoys a strong position in the religious tradition of Christianity and in modern science. Groothuis explains the vital importance of this view for Christianity. He says, "Without the correspondence view of truth, these resounding affirmations can only ring hollow. Therefore, the correspondence view of truth is not simply one of many options for Christians. It is the only biblically and logically grounded view of truth available and allowable. We neglect or deny it to our peril and disgrace. Truth decay will not be dispelled without it."[15] Alister McGrath thinks that the same can be said for modern science.

---

[13]David K. Clark, *To Know and Love God* (Wheaton, IL: Crossway, 2003), 354.

[14]John Searle, *Mind, Language and Society* (New York: Basic Books, 1998), 9.

[15]Douglas Groothuis, *Truth Decay: Defending Christianity Against the Challenges of Postmodernism* (Downers Grove, IL: InterVarsity Press, 2000), 110.

While talking about the epistemological commitments of the natural sciences, he says, "Despite all the qualifications that must be entered against our broad statement that theory must be grounded in or consistent with experimental observations, the general principle holds: scientific theories must be grounded in the real world. They are accountable to the reality they purport to represent. Ontological finality thus rests with nature itself."[16]

Nevertheless, some postmodern philosophers have taken great exception to this perspective of truth. At the heart of their objection is the concern that our mental representation and comprehension of the world may be impossible to verify and show to be accurate. As they see it, it is always possible that there is a strong disconnect between what we believe about the world and the world itself.

So, what should we make of this concern? We will get to this question and a much more lengthy discussion and treatment in chapter 6 when we deal with the issue of perception. For now, however, a brief reply is in order. To be clear, these postmodern philosophers do raise a legitimate concern. Perhaps we have all experienced situations where we thought one thing about the world, only to find out that we were not quite seeing things the way they really are. Despite this concern, however, it looks like the postmodern philosophers are overstating their case and drawing illogical conclusions. Although it is always possible that our statements about the world may not be perfectly accurate, it is foolish to say that there can be no correspondence whatsoever between statements and reality. If so, then we should continue thinking that truth statements are those that correspond to the world itself.

How Do We Identify Truth?

So far we have considered two big questions: Is anything really true? And, what is truth? Now we turn to another important question: How do we identify truth, or test truth claims? In the last section we considered three rival definitions for truth: coherence, pragmatism and correspondence. And, as we saw, coherentism and pragmatism seem to have major

---

[16]Alister E. McGrath, *A Scientific Theology*, 3 vols. (Grand Rapids: Eerdmans, 2001–2003), 2:16.

problems if they are regarded as definitions for truth. What these problems show is that these theories are insufficient ways of describing the nature of truth. This does not mean, however, that coherentism and pragmatism are of no value when it comes to testing truth claims. In fact, it can be argued that each of these is a necessary condition for truth.

The distinction between a necessary and sufficient condition was discussed in chapter 2, where we considered the Gettier problem. There we saw that a necessary condition is a condition that must be met in order for something else to exist or happen. Yet, just because necessary conditions are met does not guarantee that a given state of affairs or event will follow. A sufficient condition, by contrast, is a condition that if met will guarantee that something exists or that an event will happen. With this quick refresher on necessary and sufficient conditions, we can now better evaluate pragmatism and coherentism as tests for truth. With both of these, we saw that they identified critical aspects of truth—truth works, and truth is consistent—but ultimately failed as complete sets of criteria for truth. As such, we might think of both coherentism and pragmatism as necessary conditions for truth but not sufficient conditions for truth. In other words, for a statement to be true, it is necessary for the statement to be consistent with other things that are true and have a particular utility. But these conditions alone do not guarantee that something is true. Some examples might help make this even clearer.

Most people take it for granted that, for our beliefs to be true, they must be consistent and coherent with each other. As Groothuis notes, "For any worldview to be true, its essential tenets must be consistent with one another logically, in accordance with the laws of non-contradiction."[17] If we discover that a particular set of beliefs is not consistent or somehow contradictory, then we intuitively recognize that either one or all of the beliefs are false. Take, for example, people who claim that there are no moral standards for judging behaviors. According to them, it is foolish, arrogant or manipulative to say there is such a thing as right and wrong in an objective sense. Yet, we are surprised to find that these persons are offended and grow hostile

---

[17]Groothuis, *Truth Decay*, 97.

when they are being wronged or mistreated. They object to such behavior, protest the treatment and appeal to a particular authority to
have things set in order. There seems to be a glaring inconsistency
between these persons' claimed beliefs and their obvious behavior. On
the one hand, they claim that there is no such thing as right and wrong.
On the other hand, they revolt when wronged. Their beliefs are be-
trayed by their responses to another person's misdeeds. Either their
belief that there is no such thing as right and wrong or their response
to the misdeeds of another must be misguided and wrong. They must
choose one or the other. They cannot have their cake and eat it too.

Consider solipsism as one other example of incoherence. Solipsists
believe that nothing exists other than themselves. In other words, they
deny the existence of all physical reality—all persons and everything
outside of their own mental existence. So, consider the inconsistency
that arises when solipsists try to convince another person that solipsism
is true. If solipsism is true, then what good is it to argue with *another
person*? According to solipsism, that person does not exist. The argument
itself suggests a belief in the reality of other persons.

Other examples could be given here, but these two should be sufficient
to make the point. Coherence of ideas may not guarantee that a particular set of ideas is true. Nevertheless, for a particular set of beliefs to
be true, they must be consistent with themselves. If they fail to be consistent, then either one or all of the beliefs are false. So, coherence does
appear to be a necessary condition for truth.

The same point can also be made about pragmatism. If a particular
belief is true, then it will, at minimum, prove to be useful. Consider an
easy and obvious example. In science we tend to favor explanations that
allow us to predict a particular outcome and thus perform a particular
task. Newton's laws of motion, for example, help us to predict what will
happen when energy is exerted on a particular object. Because these
predictions come true, we can now develop weapons, create aircraft and
do many other extraordinary things. Why do we think some of Newton's
theories are true? We think this for one simple reason: they work! Like
coherentism, pragmatism may offer us a helpful way of testing truth
claims even if it is an inadequate definition for truth.

CONCLUSION

In this chapter we have maintained that, despite what some postmodern thinkers have argued, there is such a thing as objective truth and it is therefore possible to have knowledge of this truth. We have also argued that a correspondence theory of truth is the only sufficient way of defining the nature of truth. This does not mean, however, that coherentism and pragmatism have no value when it comes to truth claims. As we have shown, they are necessary conditions for truth and are, therefore, vitally important as tests for truth.

DISCUSSION QUESTIONS

1. What reason is there to think that something is true?

2. What are the various ways that truth has been defined, and how do they compare?

3. Even if we adopt a correspondence theory of truth, do coherentist and pragmatic approaches have any value for us?

5

What Are Inferences, and
How Do They Work?

So far we have considered some of the most basic and rudimentary issues within epistemology. In many cases the importance of these issues is obvious and unavoidable. For example, the question about where knowledge comes from seems to be a natural and important issue in the study of knowledge. There are, however, some issues that normally receive less attention than they rightly deserve. They may be regularly overlooked, but they are still vitally important. Such is the case with the issue of inference. We make inferences every day of our lives, and inferences play an enormous role in the accumulation of our knowledge. And yet, this is one of the biggest places where we can run into epistemic danger or error. In this chapter we will examine the nature and importance of inferences, the different kinds of inferences that we make and the various things that cause us to make inferential mistakes.

What Is an Inference?

So, what is an inference? Like the other questions we have considered in this book, this is probably not a question that we have given much consideration. In its most basic sense, an inference is the process of drawing a conclusion from a particular set of facts or experiences. In most cases, inferences allow us to draw conclusions that take us beyond the available information or evidence. We draw inferences about all kinds of things in all kinds of situations. In most cases, we take a particular fact or piece of evidence and draw a conclusion about it. Sometimes these conclu-

sions are simple and straightforward, and other times they require a bit
of interpretation or theorizing on our part. In either case, an inference
is something that we draw from an experience, piece of evidence, set of
facts or other kind of data. Perhaps figure 5.1 will help us to see how this
works. This diagram shows the way our thought moves from data to a
conclusion. It all begins with the data and then moves, via inference, to
a particular claim.

Figure 5.1. How People Form Inferences

We are not always aware when someone has made an inference. In fact,
we are often unaware even when we ourselves make inferences. This is
because the business of inferences is sometimes subtle and unannounced.
They form so quickly, and at times without conscious thought, that we may
not even realize when we have formed an inference. Yet, this is one of the
most important aspects of an argument and necessitates special attention
and evaluation. How do we spot inferences, and how can we evaluate
them? The simplest way is to start with the obvious claim or conclusion
the person is making, work back to the evidence given and then look for
the inference that connects them. Perhaps some examples will help.

Consider the teenage girl who bursts into her parents' room late one
Thursday night. Between sobs, she claims that her boyfriend, Tim, does
not love her anymore. It takes several minutes to calm her, but when she
stops sobbing, her father asks, "Why do you think that Tim doesn't love
you anymore?" Once again she begins to sob but finally manages to blurt
out, "Because he didn't call me tonight!" This example is a bit dramatic,
but it illustrates the way inferences work (see fig. 5.2).

What is the inference being made here? In short, the girl infers that
Tim's not calling *means* that he does not love her anymore. There are two
points to make about inferences from this example. First, in terms of
identifying the inference, notice how our investigative work seemed to
begin at the end with the claim and work backwards. In other words, we

began not by looking for the inference but by considering the claim itself, which was most obvious to us. In this case, we begin with the teenage girl's claim that Tim did not love her anymore. From this, we worked backwards and asked what the evidence for that claim might be. In this case her evidence was that Tim did not call. Up until this point it might be difficult to find the inference that she is making. But when we have identified the claim and the evidence, it is now easy to see the inference that she makes. In this case she infers that Tim's not calling *means* that he does not love her. This brings us to our second important lesson about inferences. In short, this example reminds us of how we can make im-

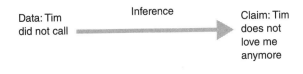

Figure 5.2. How Inferences Work

proper inferences. For example, does the fact that Tim did not call *mean* that he does not love her? Maybe, or maybe not. We must admit that it is possible that Tim's feelings for the girl have changed. But this wise father will probably try to help his daughter realize that her conclusion might not be true. Whether he realizes it or not, the father is evaluating her inference. What if there is another explanation for Tim's not calling? What if he lost his cell phone or was so tired after football practice that he fell asleep as soon as he got home? Or, perhaps Tim's mother is upset with him because of his bad grades on his report card and has taken his cell phone away. Because any of these are genuine possibilities, all of the girl's tears might be for nothing.

Consider another example. Suppose you walk into a special banquet that your employer is having for a foreign business partner. Your boss sent everyone an e-mail giving the time and the location of the event. Because he said nothing about the dress for this occasion, you assume that business casual is appropriate and appear at the event dressed accordingly. When you walk through the door, there is an awkward silence as everybody turns and looks at you. You notice two things: this is a black-tie event, and your boss looks very unhappy. Later that evening your boss pulls you aside and gives you a serious reprimand for dressing the way that you have for this event. In fact, he puts you on notice, letting you know that one more infraction of this nature will cost you your job. You apologize profusely to your boss and try to explain that you did not know how to dress. At this point, your boss criticizes you even more harshly, saying that you are lazy and irresponsible because you obviously do not check your e-mail. Unbeknownst to you, your boss sent out a second e-mail specifying the dress for the event. Nevertheless, you did not receive that e-mail because it was caught in your company's spam filter. In this case, your boss's interpretation is that you are lazy and irresponsible because you did not read his second e-mail about the dress code. But once again, does the conclusion obviously follow from the evidence? Surely there are times when employees are lazy and irresponsible. But in this case laziness and irresponsibility are not the reasons why you had not read the email. The cause of the problem was the company's spam filter.

Both of the examples given here illustrate the way inferences work but also highlight the way we can make improper inferences. Fortunately, we do not always make the wrong inference about things. There are all kinds of places where we avoid the kinds of mistakes mentioned above and infer properly. More will be said toward the end of the chapter about how to avoid these mistakes. For now, however, it is important to describe the different kinds of inferences we make.

What Kinds of Inferences Do We Make?

So far we have considered the nature of inferences and how they work in our thinking. We have seen that inferences allow us to expand our knowledge and go beyond evidence and experience to get at the meaning of things and events. It is important to note that there are various kinds of inferences and each has played an important role in human knowledge. Generally speaking, there are three different kinds of inferences that we make: deductive, inductive and abductive. Here we consider some examples of each of these and what makes them distinct.

Deductive inferences. Deduction is one important form of inference, in which we draw out what might be entailed within a concept or belief. Typically associated with Aristotle and Aristotelianism, this kind of inference sometimes employs something called a syllogism. With this, we often start with two or more premises and draw a conclusion. For example, one might argue as follows:

(1) All men are mortal.

(2) Socrates is a man.

Therefore

(3) Socrates is a mortal.

In this case, (1) and (2) are premises used to draw the conclusion of (3)—Socrates is a mortal. There are several things to notice about this kind of inference.

First, note what we learn when we arrive at (3). In one sense, (3) really does say something beyond what has already been said in (1) and (2). It tells us something specific about Socrates—he is mortal—that we may or may not have already thought about prior to arriving at that conclusion. Yet, in this case, we have not learned anything new when we arrived at (3) because (3) is already entailed within (1) and (2). To say that one idea is entailed within another idea, or combination of two ideas, is to say that the idea logically follows from the first idea. In the case of the argument given above, (3)—Socrates is a mortal—logically follows from the preceding premises:

(1) All men are mortal.

(2) Socrates is a man.

As such, (3) did not say anything new. It did clarify something that had not yet been clarified, but it did not yield any new information.

Second, despite the fact that this kind of argument did not yield any new information, note the certainty of (3) in this argument. If this argument works, it will yield an absolutely sure conclusion, even if no new information is given. But this raises an important question. What does it take for an argument like this to work? Philosophers typically note two important conditions for these kinds of arguments: validity and soundness. Validity has to do with the structure and mechanics of the argument itself. If the argument is put together in the right way and is properly structured, then the conclusion will necessarily follow. In other words, even if its conclusion is false, one can have a valid argument as long as it is structured properly. Consider the following example.

(1) All fish are blue.

(2) Nemo is a fish.

Therefore

(3) Nemo is blue.

Though the conclusion is false, this is a valid argument. Most students who are new to philosophy find this fact puzzling because it is quite obvious that Nemo is not blue. But once again, it is important to note that validity refers only to the *structure* of the argument and promises that a given conclusion follows from properly structured arguments.

The problem with the argument about Nemo is not that it is invalid. Rather, the problem is that premise (1) is not true. Because it is a valid argument, if premise (1) were true, and premise (2), then (3) would be necessarily true. So then, for a deductive argument to work, it must be structured properly (valid), and its premises must actually be true. We call deductive arguments that are valid and have true premises sound arguments. Soundness, therefore, refers to deductive arguments with true premises and valid structure. The argument given above about Socrates being a mortal is a prime example of a sound argument. Consider this argument once again.

(1) All men are mortal.

(2) Socrates is a man.

Therefore

(3) Socrates is a mortal.

In this case, the argument is valid and the premises are true. Therefore, this is a sound argument. So then, if the deductive argument is sound, the inference that it draws will be sure and certain. Therefore, when dealing with these kinds of inferences, we must pay special attention to the structure of the argument and the truthfulness of the premises.

Third, these kinds of arguments normally move from general premises to specific conclusions. In the case of the argument about Socrates, we begin with (1) *All* men are mortal. The operative word here is *all*, as it makes a categorical statement about every human being throughout history. By contrast, by the time we end with (3)—Socrates is a mortal—we have a very specific statement about one person named Socrates. In other words, in (3) we identify one particular person (Socrates) and say something very particular about him (he is a mortal). So, we might represent this with figure 5.3.

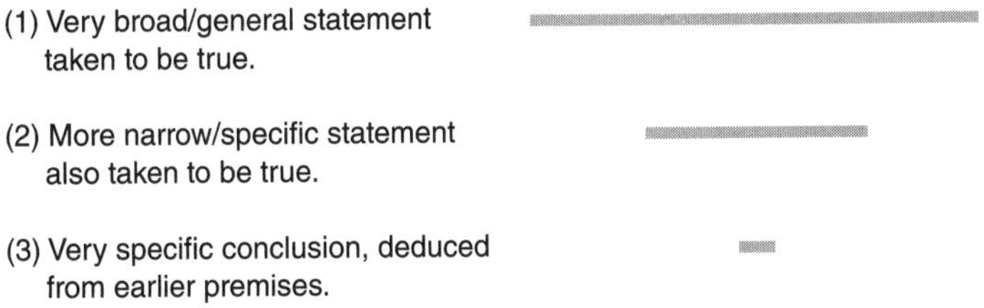

(1) Very broad/general statement
    taken to be true.

(2) More narrow/specific statement
    also taken to be true.

(3) Very specific conclusion, deduced
    from earlier premises.

Figure 5.3. Inferential Process in a Deductive Argument

In this diagram, argument, or inferential process, moves from top to bottom. We begin with a premise that is very broad and general and then move down toward a concise and specific conclusion. So again, deductive arguments move from very general premises to specific conclusions about particular objects.

Inductive inferences. In addition to deductive inferences, we also regularly employ inductive inferences in our thinking. This kind of reasoning has had an especially dominant role in our thinking from the time of Francis Bacon, who rejected deduction in favor of induction, arguing that deduction clarified things but gave us no good way of learning anything new. This kind of reasoning does not always take the official form of an argument but can still be represented in the form of an argument for the sake of clarity. If, for example, we wanted to formulate a theory about barking dogs in light of the evidence we have at our disposal, our argument, or inference, might look something like this:

(1) Every dog we know of barks.

(2) Therefore, dogs bark.

In this argument, we infer (2) from (1). If in fact every fish we know of is blue, then in all probability, all other fish are blue. Although this kind of inference might be helpful for us in our thinking and knowing, we should note that inductive inferences like these operate very differently from deductive inferences in a number of important ways.

First, notice that, unlike deductive arguments that begin with very general premises and move to particular conclusions, inductive inferences do the opposite. They begin with particular observations and then move to more general conclusions. That is, with deduction, we start with "all" and conclude with "one" (in the case above, Socrates). In the case of induction, however, we start with our experiences or knowledge of all the individual cases of a thing we have encountered and conclude with a very broad affirmation of "all." We might represent this approach with figure 5.4.

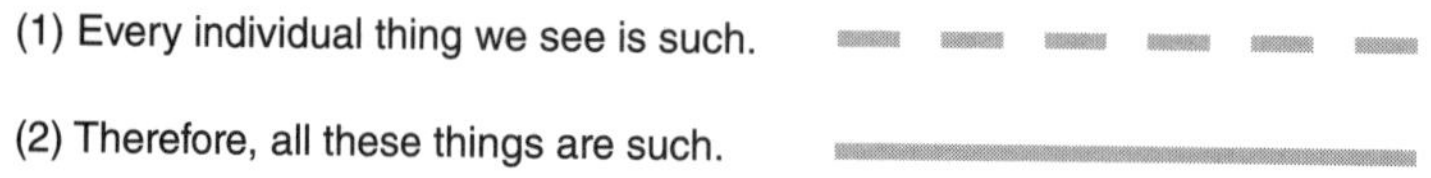

(1) Every individual thing we see is such.   ▬ ▬ ▬ ▬ ▬ ▬

(2) Therefore, all these things are such.   ▬▬▬▬▬▬▬▬▬▬▬▬▬

Figure 5.4. Inferential Process in an Inductive Argument

In this diagram, the individual lines on the top represent the individual particular things that we experience. In induction, we start with the individual things of our experience and try to account for them. The bottom line represents a conclusion we draw about all the individual things of our experience.

This idea was important to Bacon, who thought that deduction did not spend enough time focusing on the particular things that needed an explanation. He said, "There has been no one who has spent an adequate amount of time on the things themselves and on experience."[1] He also thought that deduction forces us to decide in advance what is, or is not, true, and then interpret the facts in light of the theory. Too often, he thought, we decide what we want to be true or accept what someone else has said about it before we look at what is really there and see what the evidence suggests. When we do this, we normally find that there is difficulty getting the theory and the facts to fit together. When this happens, we have to either ignore the facts or bend them to fit with what we want them to say. By contrast, he felt that induction lets the evidence gained from observation of particular things speak for itself and that theories arise naturally from these observations. He wrote, "By contrast, by our method, axioms are gradually elicited step by step, so that we reach the

---

[1]Francis Bacon, *The New Organum* (New York: Cambridge University Press, 2000), 9.

most general axioms only at the very end; and the most general axioms come out not as notional, but as well-defined, and such as nature acknowledges as truly known to her, and which live in the heart of things."[2]

This brings us to a second important distinction about the nature of inductive inferences. Unlike deductive inferences, which normally do not expand our knowledge beyond what we already know, induction gives us the ability to learn tremendous amounts of things about the world in which we live. Again, this was one of Bacon's major concerns with deduction. Offering a stinging critique of Aristotle's deductive method, he said, "This then, more or less is the condition of the traditional and received kinds of learning: barren of results, full of questions; slow and feeble in improvement; claiming perfection in the whole, but very imperfect in the parts."[3] He then added, "Such men make some emendations but little progress; they improve existing learning but do not progress to anything new."[4] In Bacon's view, the primary failure of deduction was that it started with assumptions about nature instead of investigating nature itself to see what was there. This meant that science was never able to make progress in its understanding of the world. By giving careful attention to the things of our experience and making thorough observations, Bacon thought that we could formulate accurate theories and expand our knowledge. The history of modern science seems to prove that Bacon was right in his thinking. With this methodology modern science was born and has revolutionized the world in which we live. We now know more and can do more than many ever thought possible. Indeed, induction does allow us to expand our knowledge.

There is a third aspect of induction that must be mentioned, and this one is very important. Unlike deduction, which came to sure and certain conclusions, induction can never produce absolute certainty. Instead, it produces high degrees of certitude or probability. This is because induction operates on the basis of experience. Because we can never experience every single thing that might need to be accounted for, and it is

---

[2]Ibid., 17.
[3]Ibid., 8.
[4]Ibid., 9.

always possible that we are deceived in our experiences, we can never have an absolute or complete certainty about what we affirm. Consider once again the argument given about barking dogs.

(1) Every dog we know of barks.

(2) Therefore, dogs bark.

In this argument, the conclusion that dogs bark is inferred from (1), which states that every dog we know of barks. But what if there is a dog somewhere at some place that does not bark and will never bark? If this is true, or even possibly true, then we can never have a complete certainty that (2) is true. But what if we changed (1) to state something like the following?

(1′) We have observed six billion dogs all over the world of all shapes, colors and sizes, and all of them bark.

If we substitute (1′) for (1), it would seem ridiculous not to affirm (2). Indeed, in light of (1′), it would be foolish not to affirm (2), but we must admit what kind of affirmation we are making and the degree of confidence that we can have in this affirmation. Even if (1′) is true, it is still theoretically possible that we will one day experience a dog who has not, does not and will not ever bark. Because of this, we cannot have absolute certainty about (2). We can, however, have a very high level of certitude about (2), because it is inferred from such a wide-ranging empirical base—(1′). So then, while inductive inferences may not produce absolute certainty, they can yield a very high level of confidence about our affirmations.

Abductive inferences. Finally, it is also possible to make what is called an abductive inference. With abductive inferences, we are making inferences to the best explanation of a particular phenomenon. This approach is normally associated with Charles Sanders Peirce (1839–1914), an American philosopher who gave considerable attention to scientific reasoning. He is known as the father of pragmatism, which we considered in the last chapter, and the most important developer of abduction. In some ways, abduction is very similar to normal inductive inferences in that it draws conclusions not necessarily entailed within the evidence or premises of an argument. Yet, as Duncan Pritchard has noted, abduction is unlike induction "in that it does not make appeal to a large representative set of observations. Instead . . . [it proceeds] from a single observed phenomenon to the best explanation of that phenomenon."[5] Peter Lipton offers a helpful illustration:

> When an astronomer infers that a star is receding from the earth with a specified velocity, she does this because the recession would be the best explanation of the observed red shift of the star's characteristic spectrum. When a detective infers that it was Moriarty who committed the crime, he does so because this hypothesis would best explain the fingerprints, bloodstains, and other forensic evidence. . . . The evidence will not entail that Moriarty is to blame, since it always remains possible that someone else was the perpetrator. Nevertheless, Holmes is right to make his inference, since Moriarty's guilt would provide a better explanation of the evidence than would anybody else's.[6]

Like inductive inferences, abductive inferences do not draw out an idea that is entailed within an earlier premise, so they do not yield absolute certainty. Yet, unlike induction, this approach uses a much smaller experiential basis of phenomena to make its inferences. It considers a particular phenomenon and looks for the best possible explanation for it.

Astronomers, for example, consider the data gathered from space and physics and formulate theories about how and when the universe came into existence. Although many different theories have been held throughout history, virtually all astronomers today affirm the big bang theory of the universe's beginnings. At the heart of this theory's rationale lie two important pieces of evidence: (1) cosmic background radiation and (2) the red shift of stars. There are other pieces of information that the big bang theory explains, but these two pieces of information are the most important. And the big bang theory holds such a dominant position today in astronomy precisely because it is the best explanation for these two pieces of data.

How Do We Use Inferences?

So far we have considered the nature of inference and the various kinds of inferences that we make. But how big a role do inferences play in our

---

[5]Duncan Pritchard, *What Is This Thing Called Knowledge?* (New York: Routledge, 2010), 96.
[6]Peter Lipton, "Inference to the Best Explanation," in *A Companion to the Philosophy of Science*, ed. W. H. Newton-Smith (Malden, MA: Blackwell, 2001), 184-85.

thinking, believing and knowing? Given the various domains of our lives that require us to make inferences, it is safe to say that they play an enormous role. As we have already discussed, scientists make inferences all the time about a wide variety of things. They consider a set of data and then try to develop a theory that best explains what they find. The process of formulating theories is the process of inference, and it is at the heart of the scientific enterprise.

But scientists are not the only ones who draw inferences. We draw inferences during a trial. For example, we hear that Jones was murdered by someone with a 9mm pistol around 7:30 p.m. on Wednesday. We then recall that Miller hated Jones, owned a 9mm pistol and was mysteriously missing on Wednesday at 7:30 p.m. From this, we infer that Miller murdered Jones. This kind of example might sound trivial at first, but people are convicted of crimes on a regular basis on exactly this kind of circumstantial evidence.

We also draw inferences in our relationships with other people, as in the example mentioned earlier of the teenage girl whose boyfriend did not call her. But other examples could be listed here. Consider what happens when Smith's boss does not give him a promotion. Smith takes this to *mean* that his boss does not like him very much. This might be true, but then again, it might not be true. It might mean that there is someone else more qualified than Smith for the job. Or, it could be that Smith's boss has something else in mind for this position. Either way, inferences have played a big role in what Smith has come to believe.

We can say that inference plays an important role in theology as well. Theologians engage in a similar process that requires them to draw inductive inferences. Consider what happens when theologians move from the various specific claims in the Bible about a given issue to making comprehensive statements about the issue as a whole—that is, what happens when we do systematic theology. In this case, we formulate a doctrinal statement—theological theory—in light of the detailed statements about an issue found in Scripture. In the process, theologians draw an inference as they move from specific statements in the Bible to more general systematized statements. We call these systematized statements doctrines. A classic example of this is the Christian doctrine of the Trinity. Because the Bible does not contain the word *trinity*, it was not immediately obvious to the early church that God was one in essence and three in persons. Yet, as the church wrestled with the particular statements about Christ in the Bible and considered all the evidence that needed to be considered, the doctrine of the Trinity was the most natural and obvious conclusion that could be drawn.

The fact that theology employs inductive inferences does not imply an epistemological deficiency on the part of theology. Rather, it recognizes that such inferences are a regular and unavoidable aspect of the way we as human beings put our thoughts together. In the end, the epistemological strength or weakness of a discipline depends not on whether it draws inferences but on the strength or weakness of the inference itself. When the evidence is strong and the one drawing the inference has been cautious and careful along the epistemic journey, our confidence is greatly increased.

What all this shows is that inference plays an enormous role in our thinking, believing and knowing. But why is it that we depend on inferences so much? The simple explanation is that facts often do not interpret themselves. The facts are just the facts. What they mean, however, is something completely different. Tim's not calling his girlfriend is a simple fact. What this means is something different. To get at the meaning of this fact requires interpretation. And because it is possible to interpret his not calling in a variety of different ways, we must pay special attention to the way we draw inferences.

WHY ARE INFERENCES TRICKY?

So far we have looked at a variety of different issues and questions pertaining to inferences. We have not, however, said anything about the danger and room for potential error that arises in the process of drawing inferences. If we are not careful, it is easy to draw the wrong inference and thus come to the wrong conclusion. Consider the following example. Suppose you are sitting in your living room and hear a young boy outside screaming "NO! NO! NO!" You then look out your window and see that your neighbor James is hitting his son in the face and on the body right in his own front yard. You cannot believe your eyes and immediately think to yourself that your neighbor James is a child abuser. Not knowing what to do, you call 911, and the authorities quickly arrive on the scene. After you have finished talking with the 911 dispatcher, you call people in your church and other neighbors to tell them about everything you have just seen. You ask them, "Did you know that James is a child abuser?" They say, "No. Why do you say that?" And you say, "Because I just saw him beating his son in the front yard." Let us think for a few moments about your cognitive process in coming to this conclusion. You have concluded that James is a child abuser. This conclusion is based on the experience of seeing him hitting his son in the face and on the body in his own front yard. The question is, however, does this evidence *mean* that James is a child abuser? It might, or it might not.

Now suppose the next day you find out that James's son had been out playing in the front yard and ran into a hive of bees. The bees came out in swarms and began stinging James's son all over his face and body. Unfortunately, James's son is highly allergic to bees and just a few stings would be enough to kill him. As it turned out, James heard his son screaming in the front yard and came outside to find him being stung by a swarm of bees. James then did what any father would do and began trying to help his son fight off the bees. To do this, James swatted at his son's face and his body as hard and as fast as he possibly could. What to you looked like a father beating his son was a father trying to save his son's life. But what went wrong when you made the claim that James was a child abuser? Was it the evidence? No, not really. You saw that James was hitting his son. The problem came when you inferred from this experience that it *meant* James was a child abuser. The problem, therefore, was not an evidential problem but an inferential problem.

This illustrates how drawing inferences can be fertile ground for epistemological error. And yet, because inferences are unavoidable and play such a dominant role in our thinking and understanding, should we conclude that all of our beliefs and knowledge are wrong or misguided? When thinking about inferences, we suggest that there are two extremes that should be avoided: (1) ignore inferences as if they never happened or are not important, and (2) assume that because inferences can give rise to error, knowledge is not possible. On the one hand, if we ignore the fact that we make inferences all the time and that we can make big mistakes in the process of making an inference, we are naïve and doomed to epistemological error. We should take this into consideration and learn how to make inferences properly. On the other hand, if we take a pessimistic view that all of our knowledge is tainted by inference and that therefore knowledge is impossible, we reduce ourselves to absurdity by taking a highly unrealistic view of human knowledge. One way that we can avoid making improper inferences is by taking note of the various ways that our inferences are tainted. These can be tainted in any number of ways that are easily avoidable. For example, our inferences are sometimes tainted by the biases we hold about people, places, topics and events. Other times, they are tainted by our background, education, upbringing or friends. In other words, we tend to view events and information through these lenses. Being aware of this will help us in taking a step towards being more objective in our thinking.

CONCLUSION

This chapter explored a wide variety of issues that pertain to inferences. We looked at what inferences are, how they function and the different kinds of inferences that we draw. We have also noted how important inferences are and how they can lead us into epistemological error. Nevertheless, when we take note of the potential hazards in our thinking, we believe that these pitfalls can be avoided. More on this will be discussed in chapter 8 when we deal with the epistemological virtues.

DISCUSSION QUESTIONS

1. What is an inference, and what role do inferences play in our apprehension of reality?
2. How does deduction work, and how certain can we be about deductive conclusions?
3. What is an inductive inference, and how does this differ from deduction?
4. How is abduction similar to and different from induction?
5. Why do we need inferences, and why are they tricky?

6

What Do We Perceive?

SO FAR WE HAVE CONSIDERED SEVERAL important issues that pertain to our knowledge. In chapter 3 we considered the sources of knowledge and there showed how experience is one of the most important sources of our knowledge as human beings. We know, for example, that the sun has risen today because we look into the sky and see it and feel it shining down on us. I know that my wife is speaking to me because I hear her voice and see her lips moving. I walk in the door to my house and know that dinner will be ready soon because I can smell the ribs in the oven coming to a finish. In all these cases, we claim to know based on experience of a particular kind: perception. In each of these cases we use different senses to make different kinds of perceptions.

There are two important questions that we will consider in this chapter. What are the various kinds of perceptions that we have? And second, what is a perception? Or put another way, how well do our perceptions tell us about the external world outside of our minds? On the face of things it may look like we should deal with the second question first. After all, we should want to know exactly what perception is before we consider the different kinds that we have. Yet, there are reasons for ordering our presentation the way we have. First, determining the various kinds of perceptions that we have is a much easier task than determining the nature of perception itself. Second, a survey of the kinds of perceptions that we have will help us later in dealing with the various theories of perception, but noting the kinds of perceptions we have will also raise many of the important questions that a given theory will have to address. Because of this, we will deal with the kinds of perceptions first and then deal with the more difficult question of the nature of perception. For now, we will take it that perceptions are the means by which we understand the world around us.

What Kinds of Perceptions Do We Have?

As human beings, we have perceptions about all kinds of things. Because of this, it will be helpful to identify some broad categories of perception. On the simplest level, we could say that there are two general categories: mental perceptions and physical perceptions. Mental perceptions refer to the awareness of things that we gain not by sight or sound but by thinking, reflecting on and remembering our thoughts. It is often the case for us that while reflecting on a conversation or past event we become aware of something we had not seen before when the original event or conversation took place. While it is true that these kinds of perceptions depend on prior physical perceptions, they are still different from them in ways that warrant separate treatment and consideration. In many ways this category of perception is much easier to deal with from an epistemological standpoint than are physical perceptions. As we will see, it is possible that we can be mistaken in our physical perceptions. But when it comes to mental perceptions, our confidence is much stronger. For example, I may be able to doubt whether or not the chair in my office is there or merely an illusion. But I cannot doubt that it *seems to me* to be in my office. Likewise, when I reflect on a past event and begin to realize something about that event that I had not previously realized, I cannot doubt that I am thinking about that event.

The more difficult task, from an existing logical standpoint, is accounting for our physical perceptions, or the perceptions we have via the five senses: seeing, touching, hearing, smelling and tasting. Let us start with an assumption that virtually all human beings have about these kinds of sense perceptions. When we see something or hear something, most of us believe to have direct and immediate access to the object that is seen or heard. In this view, perception is a kind of direct and immediate relationship between you the perceiver and the object that you are perceiving. We will give this basic assumption a full treatment in the next section on theories of perception because it represents a common-sense view of perception known as direct realism. We mention it here in brief because it provides an excellent starting point for considering the kinds of perceptions we have via the five senses.

In this view, we tend to think that perception is a two-part relationship between the perceiver and the perceived. But as we think about it for a moment, we quickly realize that there may be much more involved than this. In fact, in some cases with some of the senses, it looks like perception could actually be a three-part relationship between the perceiver, the perceived and some sort of intermediary object. To make this clearer, let us consider what happens as we perceive things with the five senses.

Consider what happens when we see a particular object. Most of us assume that our sight of the particular object gives us direct and immediate access to the object itself, such that we are really seeing the object. If that were true, then visual perception would be a two-part relationship between the object and perceiver. Yet, in some cases, it looks like this is too simplistic and thus potentially wrong. Take, for example, what happens when we look at the sun or a star. In the case of the sun we are looking at the object as it was approximately eight minutes ago, but not as it is right now. With stars, this is even more pronounced and significant, because the light we see in our perception at present represents the star as it was years ago or even hundreds or thousands of years ago. But if that is true, it is always possible that we are looking at stars that no longer exist. What this suggests to us is that visual perception may not be as direct and immediate as we first think. This also suggests that visual perception is a three-part relationship between the object, the light waves and the perceiver.

The same kind of observation could be made with regard to hearing and smelling. Again, we normally believe that when we hear a car approaching, we are hearing the car itself. We also believe that when we smell cookies baking, we smell the cookies themselves. But consider what happens in the case of sound. I have vivid memories of playing center field for my high school baseball team and standing in the outfield waiting for the ball to be hit to me. As any centerfielder can tell you, you will always see the ball hit about one second before you hear the ball clank off the hitter's bat. This is because sound travels much slower than light, and thus there is a lag in time between events and their sounds. As in the case of visual perceptions, therefore, it looks like our sound perceptions are not as direct and immediate as we tend to assume, and that these kinds of perceptions detail a three-part relationship between object, sound waves and the perceiver. Likewise, this also seems true when it comes to smelling. When we smell the cookies baking in the oven, we are smelling the aroma given off by the cookies in the oven as they are cooking, but we do not immediately and directly encounter the cookies themselves.

Unlike seeing, hearing and smelling, the perceptions of touch and taste seem to be more direct and immediate, and thus are good examples of a two-part kind of perception. For example, when you reach out and touch your friend's hand, you are really touching his hand. This kind of perception is direct and immediate and does not require some third object like sound or light waves to make it possible. Similarly, when you put a cookie in your mouth and taste the sweetness of sugar and chocolate, it seems as though your perception is again direct and immediate. Yet, even in these cases there are some reasons to think that there is more involved in these kinds of perceptions. Consider what happens when you dip your hand in a bowl of water and perceive it to be cold. Is it actually cold? According to empiricist philosophers, the answer is no; coldness is in the mind of the one perceiving the water but not in the water itself. A simple thought experiment will help illustrate why empiricist philosophers like John Locke and others would take this view. Imagine that you have three bowls of water in front of you: one burning hot, one lukewarm and one ice cold. Now suppose that you let your left hand soak in the bowl of hot water while also letting your right hand soak in the bowl of cold water for approximately two minutes. Then, after two minutes, you take both hands out of their bowls and place them both in the middle bowl that is lukewarm. To the left hand, which has been soaking in hot water, the middle bowl will feel icy cold. To the right hand, which has been soaking in very cold water, the middle bowl will feel burning hot. Or, in the case of tasting, consider what happens when we taste a particular flavor. In most cases, taste is rather simple and straightforward.

But at other times, it seems as though even this kind of perception can be tainted. When I drink orange juice, for example, after just brushing my teeth, the taste of orange juice itself is misrepresented. Empiricist philosophers argue that this suggests that sensations such as hotness, coldness, sweetness or sourness are in the mind of the perceiver and not in the objects themselves.

Generally speaking, these are the kinds of mental and physical perceptions that we have on a daily basis. Given the questions that arise regarding the directness, immediacy and reliability of these perceptions, it is no wonder that philosophers and scientists have questioned this common-sense view of perception, in favor of other theories of perception. These considerations serve as a helpful backdrop to the various theories of perception to which we now turn.

WHAT ARE SOME THEORIES OF PERCEPTION?

Here we consider a question that perhaps many people have never considered. What happens in perception, or put another way, what is perception? Numerous theories have been put forward, but epistemologists put these theories into three general categories: direct realism or naïve realism, indirect realism or representationalism and phenomenalism or antirealism.

Direct realism. Much of what we have been describing in the preceding section about the kinds of perceptions that we have fits well with the direct realist theory of perception. In this theory, perception is thought to give the perceiver direct and immediate access to the objects of perception themselves. But this is not everything that can or should be said about direct realism. This theory is called a realist theory because it affirms the real existence of the object of perceptions which exist outside of the perceiver's mind even while being unperceived. In other words, this view maintains that rocks and trees continue to exist even if we are not around to perceive them, and they continue to exist even after a given perception of them has come to an end. In short, this view is a realist view because it affirms the real existence of these objects in the external world. We call this direct realism because of the directness and immediacy of the access to external objects which are given in perception. Also, this theory holds that our perceptions of the world are caused by events and objects outside of our minds. For example, the reason I perceived a sharp pain in my arm this morning is because I received a flu shot. In this case, the perception is caused by an object in the external world which acted on me and my senses. This theory is sometimes referred to as a causal theory of perceptions.

To be sure, this theory of perception has much to recommend it. Among other things, it seems to be based on a strong basis of common-sense thinking about our perceptions. Rarely, if ever, do we think that we are not seeing things the way they really are in the world. For the vast majority of our sense perceptions, it does seem that what we see is what is really there. And if what we see is not what is really there, then why is it that so many of our judgments about the physical and external world turn out to be reliable judgments? For example, if I drive down the road in my car and see another car in the opposing lane swerve into my lane at breakneck speed, I would be a fool not to hit my brakes or swerve out of the way. If I did not swerve or hit my brakes, I would probably be in a crash and could lose my life. In this case, my visual perceptions give me real and true information about what is happening. As a result of these perceptions, I am able to make a reliable judgment about my course of action. Likewise, when I walk into my house and smell the aroma of rotisserie chicken cooking, I am properly informed by this perception that we are having chicken for dinner tonight. What these considerations show is that there is something basically true about the direct realist theory of perception.

Yet, as we saw above while considering the kinds of perceptions that we have, it seems that the direct realist theory of perception does not tell the whole story. In truth, it sometimes seems as though our perceptions are not as direct and straightforward as this theory would suggest. And, as we have seen, it does not seem to account for the various ways that our perceptions can be tainted by other factors. Specifically, this theory does not take into account the many physical and contextual factors that affect our perceptions. In the case of the three water bowls mentioned above, the lukewarm bowl feels hot to the right hand because that hand has been soaking in cold water. And it feels ice cold to the left hand because that hand has been soaking in hot water. The reason the orange juice tastes odd is because of the lingering taste of toothpaste. What all of this means is that while direct realism gives us a partial account of the real world, it does not tell the whole story. Because this theory assumes that things are exactly the way they appear to us in our perceptions, this theory is sometimes referred to as naïve realism.

Indirect realism or representationalism. A second theory of perception might be labeled as either representationalism or indirect realism and is normally traced back to Locke. He said, "Whatsoever the mind perceives in itself, or is the immediate object of perception, fault, or understanding, that I call *idea*."[1] In other words, for Locke, what we directly encounter in a perception is the idea formed in the mind from the senses, and not the object itself. So, perception of the external world is indirect and representational in nature.

Like direct realism, indirect realism is a realist theory of perception because it also affirms the real existence of external objects outside the mind. It differs, however, in thinking that our apprehension of these objects in perception is direct and immediate, and thus it is referred to as indirect realism. Jonathan Dancy notes the similarity and difference of these two perspectives. He says:

> The dispute between the direct realist and the indirect realist concerns the question of whether we are ever directly aware of the existence and nature of the physical objects. Both, as realists, agree that the physical objects we see and touch are able to exist and retain some of their properties when unperceived. But the indirect realist asserts that we are never directly aware of physical objects; we are only indirectly aware of them in virtue of a direct awareness of an intermediary object (variously described as an idea, sense-datum, precept or appearance).[2]

Labeling the perspective representationalism, Louis Pojman describes the process involved in this model of perception. In this account, perceptions begin with objects or events in the world, which are then collected by the sense organs, which in turn give signals to the brain. These signals

[1]John Locke, *An Essay Concerning Human Understanding* (London: Penguin, 1997), book 2, chap. 8.
[2]Jonathan Dancy, *Introduction to Contemporary Epistemology* (Malden, MA: Blackwell, 1985), 145.

are then processed as a brain event, which leads to nonphysical ideas in the mind.[3] He offers a helpful chart (fig. 6.1) to illustrate the way perceptions represent the external world to the mind.[4]

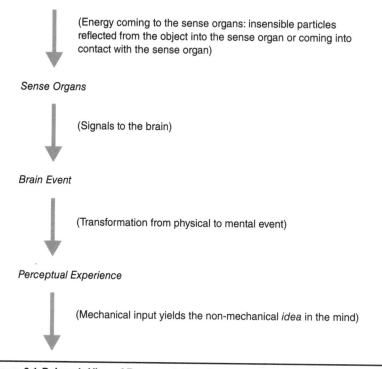

Objects and Events in the Real World

(Energy coming to the sense organs: insensible particles reflected from the object into the sense organ or coming into contact with the sense organ)

Sense Organs

(Signals to the brain)

Brain Event

(Transformation from physical to mental event)

Perceptual Experience

(Mechanical input yields the non-mechanical *idea* in the mind)

Figure 6.1. Pojman's View of Representationalism

So then, in a representationalist account of perception, we do not have direct and immediate access to the world. Rather, we apprehend the world as it is represented to us indirectly through the senses and our ideas that are formulated from the sense data. We do not experience things themselves but the images or representations of them.

As we have already seen, Locke argued that perception gives us indirect access to the external world through mental representations he called ideas. He is also known, however, for an important distinction

---

[3]Louis P. Pojman, *What Can We Know? An Introduction to the Theory of Knowledge* (Belmont, CA: Wadsworth, 2001), 67-68.
[4]Ibid.

between the kinds of qualities that we experience in objects. He called these primary qualities and secondary qualities. For Locke, a primary quality is a quality that is in the object itself and cannot be removed from it. He says, "Qualities thus considered in bodies are, first such as are utterly inseparable from the body, in one estate so ever it be; such as in all the alterations and changes it suffers, all the force can be used upon it, it constantly keeps. . . . These I call original or primary qualities."[5] Examples of primary qualities would include things like mass, number, solidarity and bulk. In other words, the qualities of being a physical thing or one thing are qualities that are in the objects themselves.

By contrast, a secondary quality is a quality that gives rise to a particular kind of sensation in us and does not genuinely reflect the object in the external world. For Locke, these qualities merely give rise to the sensations that we have about the object. He says, "Such qualities, which in truth are nothing in the objects themselves, but powers to produce various sensations in us by their primary qualities . . . these I call secondary qualities."[6] Examples of these kinds of qualities would include blue, red, soft, hot or cold. These types of qualities, Locke thought, were not really in the objects themselves but in our perceptions of them. A short word of caution is in order here, as it is easy to misunderstand what Locke is saying. Locke is not suggesting that secondary qualities are completely mental constructs. He does argue that the object in question, which is perceived to be blue by us, has something in it that gives rise to bluish sensations. Nevertheless, whatever it is in the object that gives rise to bluish sensations is not itself actually blue. Rather, when this quality in the object that gives rise to bluish sensations is perceived by you and me, it is always perceived as blue. What Locke and other empiricists like him argue is that the mind perceives blue as it infers blueness from the experience of the objects themselves.

Like direct realism, this perspective has both strengths and weaknesses. On the positive side, this view clearly accounts for the way our comprehension of the external world might be mediated by mental processes or even tainted by other factors. It is true that we are sometimes

---

[5]Locke, *Essay Concerning Human Understanding*, book 2, chap. 9.
[6]Ibid., book 2, chap. 10.

mistaken about the things that we think that we see or hear. For example, perhaps we have all been to a restaurant buffet where we saw a nice piece of meat that looked juicy and succulent. After putting the meat on our plate and returning to our table, we find that the meat now appears gray and tough. Whether we knew it or not, we were enticed into eating the meat because of the way it appeared while still on the buffet. But while in the buffet line, the meat sits under red lighting, which gives the meat a different—and in this case better—appearance than it would have otherwise had. In this case, the appearance of the meat is tainted by the light that shines on it.

Despite whatever benefit indirect realism may have, many epistemologists note a major problem with this account of perception. First, it seems counterintuitive. Each of us sees things and feels confident that we are seeing what is really there. When, for example, I see the tree in front of me, I always think that I am really seeing the tree. So, no matter how well indirect realism accounts for the various ways we can be deceived in our thinking about our perceptions, it is plagued by the persuasive force of common sense. Second, if this perspective is true, then it seems that we can never be sure about anything that is presented to us through our perceptions. If we do not encounter the objects of the external world directly but only encounter them indirectly through the sensations and ideas that represent them, then how do we know that things really are the way our sensations and ideas suggest they are? The indirect realist might respond by saying we can have confidence in the representations because they are caused by the external objects of the world. But this seems to be an insufficient basis to guarantee that our ideas truly reflect the objects outside our minds, because what we end up seeing, hearing, tasting, and so on has gone through an elaborate mental process that only represents something outside the mind. How do we know the representation is right?

To illustrate this problem, we might consider what it would be like to live life inside a good flight simulator. Inside this simulator, we are constantly given visual and spatial indicators about things outside the simulator. We see clouds, runways, birds and raindrops. We also feel the movement of the plane as wind gusts hit the plane, forcing our bodies to think that we are really being moved by wind gusts outside of the plane. But are these really happening, and do these representations truly reflect the world outside the simulator? Unless we can step outside the simulator to see the world directly, we will never know. This seems to be the problem with indirect realism. According to this view, we never have direct access to the world, but only indirectly perceive the sensations and ideas in the mind that represent the external world. These representations might give genuine reflections of the external world. But then again, they might not. This view naïvely assumes a reliable correspondence between the objects of the world and our ideas of them.

Phenomenalism or antirealism. There is one final category of views on perception known as phenomenalism or antirealism. According to this view, perception is a phenomenon of the mind which is not necessarily connected to the world itself. To be clear, phenomenologists and antirealists do not necessarily deny the existence of the external world, as metaphysical idealists would be inclined to do. Nevertheless, in their view, perception is not caused directly by external objects outside the mind. Rather, perception itself has to do with data drawn from the senses and the internal mental processes, such that knowledge is a mental construct of the individual's mind. As a result, this view sees a radical disconnect between mind and reality. As Jack Crumley II notes, this understanding of perception "denies that we should think of perception as involving mind-independent objects at all. Rather, physical objects are identified in some way with our sensations."[7] In other words, this view goes beyond indirect realism by emphasizing the role the mind plays in interpreting the data from the senses. In this view we perceive what the mind gives us. Thus, this view is much bolder than indirect realism because our sensations tell us nothing about the way things are in the world outside our minds.

At first blush, it might be hard to see how this is any different from indirect realism or representationalism. This is because they are very closely related. Both indirect realism and phenomenalism argue that perception does not give us direct access to the external world. But what makes phenomenalism different and more radical than indirect realism

---

[7]Jack S. Crumley II, *An Introduction to Epistemology* (Mountain View, CA: Mayfield, 1999), 270.

is the fact that, with phenomenalism, external objects do not dictate what we will perceive. This view is more extreme than indirect realism because it no longer assumes a real correspondence between objects in the world and the ideas in our minds.

Like indirect realism, this view has no problem accounting for the many times and places where our perceptions fail to properly reflect the world as it is. But, despite this, most philosophers—and most people in general—find this view problematic. There are two primary problems that we must note. First, what this perspective affirms is counterintuitive. The impressions we get from the world around us about its nature and detail are so strong that this theory of perception is hard to take seriously. We may very well have to grant that things can taint our perception such that we fail to see something at a given moment directly. Despite that, however, all our interactions with the world we live in are predicated on our ability to see what is really there. So, it is difficult to see how this perspective on perception is right.

Second, this account is challenged strongly by the advances made in modern science. If, for example, phenomenalism is right, then we should not be able to do most of the things that we do in the natural sciences. Consider the fact that we have been successful in putting human beings on the moon. This project required incredible precision and planning on the part of scientists as they considered the laws of physics. If their measurements and calculations had been off by even a slight margin, such accomplishments would have been impossible. If their calculations had not been exactly right, then we would have launched people off into the great expanse of space and they would have been lost forever. Instead, however, these astronauts arrived safely on the moon and returned to Earth to tell about it. All of this would have been impossible if our perceptions about the external world told us nothing about the way things are outside of our minds. In short, it seems as though modern science itself would be impossible if phenomenalism were true.

RETURN TO DIRECT REALISM?

Where does this leave us, and which theory of perception is correct? It is hard to deny that our perceptions are sometimes tainted and that we fail to see things (or smell, taste, touch or hear) as they are. To deny this would be dishonest. As we saw at the beginning of the chapter, there are too many examples of times when something like this is going on in our perceptions. These difficulties have led some philosophers to affirm either indirect realism or phenomenalism. These perspectives have some advantages over direct realism because they suggest that we do not perceive things directly. Nevertheless, we have also seen that each of these perspectives on perception comes with some fatal problems. Phenomenalism takes what many consider to be an absurd position in that it suggests that we never know anything about the external world. All we know are our perceptions, which are not caused by objects outside the mind. This position is countered by our strong and persuasive common-sense intuitions and the successes of modern science.

Indirect realism seems to strike a middle ground between direct realism and phenomenalism by claiming we have indirect access to the external world with our mental representations, which are caused by the objects outside the mind. In this account, we know our sense data directly and the external world indirectly. But as we have seen, it is hard to see how we can ever be confident that our mental world squares with the external world. In other words, if indirect realism is right, how do we know that we know anything about the world itself, because we never have direct access to the external world?

Because of these concerns, many philosophers have returned to some form of direct realism. This does not mean, however, that they have rehashed what was said before. Instead, they have embraced a perspective that once again affirms a direct encounter with the external world but at the same time acknowledges the various factors that might cause us to misapprehend reality. Here is what we can and cannot say about our perceptions.

First, aside from times when deception or hallucination takes place, it does seem that our perceptions are caused by the objects outside of our minds. If this is the case, then it seems that we have access to things outside our minds and there is at least some sense in which our perceptions of the external world are direct and immediate. When a ball, for example, strikes me on the head, it is safe to say that I have direct and immediate access to the ball itself. After all, in this case I am in direct contact with the ball itself, not just the sense data of the ball. When I see my wife walk through the door of my office to bring me lunch, I see her and not just a bundle of sensations about her. In the case of the cookies I smell cooking in the oven, it seems that even here we are justified is saying that I have direct access to something about the cookies. Perhaps it is the aroma of the cookies and not the cookies themselves. But I am still experiencing something about the cookies that is caused by the cookies. Thus, most of us are still inclined to think that our perceptions give us some kind of direct access to the world around us.

Having said that, this does not mean that we have to be naïve about our perceptions, as if we have to think that what we see is what we will necessarily get. As some scientific experiments and a little reflection show us, there are various ways that our perceptions can be wrong. We have briefly hinted at a few of these in this chapter. So, while direct realism seems to give the best account of the nature of our perceptions, it is still a possibility that some of these perceptions can be wrong. Generally speaking, we can trust our perceptions, but we must not be naïve about the potential epistemological pitfalls that can lead to error.

Given the strengths and weaknesses of each theory of perception, we may never be able to say which theory is absolutely correct. We may, however, be able to adopt a methodology that allows us to take the strengths of each theory into account. In a wide variety of intellectual disciplines—such as philosophy, theology, sociology and science—much attention has been given to developing a methodology that will allow for genuine knowledge of the external world while also noting the potential for perceptual and cognitive error. This approach is described in various ways, but it most often is referred to as critical realism. When applied to the issue of perception, this approach holds that we can apprehend the external world itself (following the intuitions of direct realism) but can also be misled by both external and internal factors (heeding the warnings of indirect realism). Though it is a genuine form of realism, it emphasizes a need for critical assessment of our perceptions, beliefs and truth claims. It holds that we see the real world, but we might not see it exactly the way it is and should thus shun the naïveté of direct realism.

Later, in chapter 8, we will look at what is often called the epistemological virtues. There we will explore in more detail how it is that we might go about being critical in our mental engagement with the world itself. When we function with these kinds of mental virtues, we go a long way toward making sure that we are not misled by our perception of the world.

Conclusion

In this chapter we considered the issue of perception. We looked at the different kinds of perceptions that we have and at different theories of perception. Reflection and scientific evidence suggest that it is possible for some of our perceptions to be wrong, but this does not mean that we must embrace phenomenalism or indirect realism. In the next chapter, we explore the issue of justification.

DISCUSSION QUESTIONS

1. What is perception, and how sure can we be about perceptions?

2. What are the different kinds of perceptions that we have?

3. What does direct realism affirm, and what are its strengths and weaknesses?

4. How does indirect realism differ from direct realism?

5. What does phenomenalism affirm, and what problems does it have?

7

Do We Need Justification?

Now that we have dealt with questions about the nature of knowledge, truth, sources of knowledge and much more, we turn to the issue of justification. In this chapter we will look at a variety of significant questions. First, what does it mean to be justified in believing something? We believe all kinds of things, and surely some of these beliefs are wrong. It would seem as though we are justified in some beliefs but not in others. So, what is the difference? Second, do we need epistemic justification to be rational in believing what we do? In this chapter we will look briefly at two different approaches—internalism and externalism—and how each answers this question. Third, how are our beliefs structured? Historically speaking, epistemologists have argued in favor of two basic models of justification: foundationalism and coherentism. And finally, what should we think about justification? Here we will argue for a modified approach that takes important lessons from several perspectives.

What Does It Mean to Be Justified?

Before we get to some of the more debated points about the issue of justification, let us first consider what it means to be justified. To be clear, what we are dealing with here is not a theological issue about the process of salvation. Rather, we are dealing with epistemological issues relating to the rationality of our beliefs. In this sense, justification refers to a person having reasons or evidence for his beliefs. To help us better understand what this means, consider two beliefs that your friend Bob might hold. Belief (A) is Bob's belief that his wife, Mary, loves Bob very much. Belief (B) is Bob's belief that his boss does not like him very much. As it turns out, Bob holds belief (A) for a number of reasons. Mary has been faithful to Bob over all the years, constantly shows tenderness and affection for Bob and tells Bob on a daily basis how much she loves him. Because of all these things, we say that Bob has justification for believing that Mary really does love him. Unlike belief (A), however, Bob does not have any reasons for believing (B). Bob's boss has never been unkind or critical toward Bob and has given Bob plenty of opportunities to advance in his career and do the things that he most wants to do. In fact, his boss has had nothing but positive things to say about Bob's performance. Yet, Bob thinks the way that he does about his boss despite the evidence. As such, belief (B)—that his boss does not like him very much—is an unjustified belief.

What is the basic difference between belief (A) and belief (B)? We consider belief (A) to be a justified belief because it is supported by evidence and good reasons. And more specifically, because of the evidence for (A), we would expect Bob to believe (A). Knowing what we know about (A), when Bob tells us he believes (A), we can easily see why he would believe it. By contrast, we consider belief (B) to be an irrational belief due to the lack of evidence and presence of counterevidence. When Bob affirms (A), we see this as a rational belief and therefore say that he is justified in (A). Bob also believes that his boss does not like him very much, but there is no good reason or evidence to support this particular belief. So then, given the information that we have about belief (B), we find it surprising and puzzling that Bob affirms (B). We see this as irrational and unjustified. Justification, therefore, has to do with being rational about our beliefs.

At this point, it is important to distinguish between a belief being justified and a belief being true. One can have all kinds of justification for a particular belief, yet the belief still may be false or misguided. For example, Bob may be rational and justified in believing (A)—that Mary loves him very much—and this belief could still be false. It is possible that Mary's displays of love and affection toward Bob are merely a show to deceive him in an effort to inherit his fortune after his death. It could be the case that Mary does not love Bob, but Bob would still be justified in believing that she does given the evidence he has that supports that belief. As we can see, then, justification does not address whether or not a belief is true. Rather, it merely counts the belief as being rational and justified when it is supported by evidence and good reason.

DO WE NEED EVIDENCE AND GOOD REASONS FOR OUR BELIEFS?

Do we need the kind of justification described above in order for our beliefs to be counted as rational? Or, perhaps more precisely, do we need evidence and good reason for our beliefs to be counted as rational? For most of Western history, philosophers have assumed the need for evidential justification, but it became even more pronounced during the Enlightenment. In recent years, however, some epistemologists have disagreed and argued that people can be rational in their beliefs even if they do not have reasons or evidence for them.

Internalism. On a most basic level, internalists believe that some kind of justification is needed for our beliefs if we are to be counted as rational. They claim that we have an epistemic obligation or duty to have good reasons to hold the beliefs that we hold.[1] This justification normally takes the form of evidence or good reasons. This view is called internalism because it claims that people have internal mental access to the evidence or arguments that support their beliefs, even though they might not be currently aware of this evidence. In other words, through internal introspection people can be aware of what justifies the belief and therefore should not be ignorant of the reasons in favor of the belief. As Louis Pojman notes:

> Internalism stresses having reasons for one's beliefs that ground or justify those beliefs . . . your "having reasons" for your belief is generally interpreted as your being able to access those reasons, be able to recall them from memory, to cite them when questioned, and to use them as premises in arguments. You are able to determine by reflection alone whether a given belief is justified for you.[2]

---

[1]This is sometimes referred to as epistemic deontology. *Deontos* is the Greek word for "duty."
[2]Louis P. Pojman, *What Can We Know? An Introduction to the Theory of Knowledge* (Belmont, CA: Wadsworth, 2001), 136.

So then, according to internalists, people are not justified in their beliefs unless they have access to and awareness of the reasons that support their beliefs.

To see how this might work, let us revisit the illustration given above about Bob and the two beliefs that he has about his wife and his boss—(A) and (B). Bob believes (A)—that Mary loves him—and has good reasons for believing this. She tells him she loves him and constantly showers him with affection. Internalists would consider this belief to have justification. Bob, however, also believes (B)—that his boss does not like him—but does not have good reasons for thinking this. According to internalists, this is not a justified belief.

Perhaps one other example will help us see the point that internalists are making. Consider Shelley, who also has two different beliefs. To avoid confusing her beliefs with Bob's beliefs, we will call Shelley's beliefs (C) and (D). (C) is Shelley's belief that her boyfriend, Jim, will propose to her this weekend. (D) is her belief that God exists. When asked by her friends why she believes (C), Shelley immediately rattles off the evidence that supports this belief. She tells them that Jim recently went to the jewelry store and looked at engagement rings, they have had many late-night conversations about getting married and they have a romantic evening planned at the finest restaurant in town this Saturday night. Surely, Jim must have something planned. Given the evidence that supports (C), internalists would say that Shelley is justified in believing (C). By contrast, when her friends ask her why she believes that God exists, Shelley does not have much to say. She pauses for a moment and then says, "I don't know. I just believe it." The fact that Shelley does not know why she believes in God does not mean that it is not true or that there are in fact no good reasons for believing this. Indeed, a large number of Christian theists could come to Shelley's aid and provide her with all kinds of reasons and arguments that support her belief in God's existence. In this case, the concern is not that such reasons do not exist but that Shelley does not have access to those reasons or arguments at the moment she is asked why she believes in God.

According to internalists, because she does not have access to the evidence and arguments that support (D), Shelley is not justified in believing

(D). Her belief (C) is like Bob's belief (A), given the fact that both are supported by evidence and good reasons. But Shelley's belief (D) is like Bob's belief (B): both are thought to be unjustified beliefs by internalists because neither Bob nor Shelley can positively support those beliefs with good reasons and evidence. Yet, as we compare (B) and (D) with each other, we quickly note that there is a difference between these two beliefs. For example, when we evaluate Shelley's belief in (D), internalists label this unjustified because Shelley does not have cognitive access to the reasons and evidence that support it. Similarly, (B) is considered to be unjustified for the same reason. But, as we think about (B) a little bit more, we see that it has an even bigger problem than (D). In the case of (B), it not only lacks positive evidence that supports it but also is countered by other evidence which seems to disprove it. So, while (B) and (D) both lack positive evidence, (B) seems to be a more problematic belief given the fact that it is countered and disproven by other evidence. Nevertheless, even though Bob's belief (B) is a more problematic belief than Shelley's belief (D), internalists would consider both (B) and (D) to be unjustified beliefs given the fact that Bob and Shelley do not have access to the reasons and evidence that support them. And so, for internalism, justified beliefs are those that the believer has good reasons or support for, and unjustified beliefs are those for which the believer lacks this kind of support.

Internalism has been taught or implied by most philosophers over the course of Western history and has taken many different forms. *Evidentialism* is perhaps the most basic and common form of internalism. In short, evidentialists claim that individual knowers have a responsibility to make sure that they believe what they believe on the basis of evidence. Moreover, if a belief cannot be supported by evidence, the belief must be rejected. Historians of philosophy normally point to an essay written in the nineteenth century by W. K. Clifford, "The Ethics of Belief," as expressing this position well. Clifford famously wrote, "It is wrong always, everywhere, and for anyone, to believe anything upon insufficient evidence."[3] You will notice in this quote that Clifford uses the word

---

[3]W. K. Clifford, "The Ethics of Belief," in *Philosophy and Choice*, ed. Kit R. Christensen (Mountain View, CA: Mayfield, 1999), 144. Clifford's essay has been widely read and reprinted since 1879, when it first appeared in his *Lectures and Essays* (Macmillan).

wrong to describe what happens when a person believes on the basis of insufficient evidence. As he makes clear immediately, he thinks it is wrong in a moral sense to have these kinds of beliefs:

> If a man, holding a belief which he was taught in childhood or persuaded of afterwards, keeps down and pushes away any doubts which could arise about it in his mind, purposely avoids the reading of books and the company of men that call in question or discuss it, and regards as impious those questions which cannot easily be asked without disturbing it—the life of that man is one long sin against mankind.[4]

On this account, both Bob in believing (B) and Shelley in believing (D) are not only unjustified in these beliefs but also immoral for holding them.

The strength of this position comes from the fact that most of us do have justified beliefs well supported by evidence and reason. When our beliefs lack this kind of support, we are normally less confident in those beliefs. Yet, many philosophers believe that Clifford's standard is too high. It has been pointed out that his statement that it is "always wrong to believe anything based upon insufficient evidence" is self-defeating, as it does not have sufficient evidence to justify it. His statement implies that one must be certain before one can be justified. However, such certainty is rarely attained. (We will examine the question of certainty in chapter 10.) By rejecting Clifford we are not abandoning evidentialism, but we might seek a less restrictive version of it.

The reason internalist forms of justification have had such a dominant role in our thinking about justification for so long is that internalism forces us to evaluate our beliefs and be reasonable about what we affirm. Because none of us want to believe things that are untrue, it is understandable that internalism would be popular among philosophers. Nevertheless, some philosophers today are inclined to think that this approach to justification is wrong. These philosophers take a position called externalism.

Externalism. Unlike internalism, externalism is the position that says it is not necessary for Shelley to have access to the reasons in evidence that support a given belief. In fact, externalists claim that many of our

---

[4]Ibid.

beliefs cannot be justified. The reasons and evidence may very well lie outside of the believer's mind or be external to the believer's cognitive grasp. Alvin Plantinga says that the externalist "holds that warrant need not depend on factors relevantly internal to the cognizer; warrant depends or supervenes upon properties to some of which the cognizer may have no special access, or even no epistemic access at all."[5] A classic example of a kind of belief often cited by externalists as not needing justification is memory. I depend on my memories as a faculty that recalls things I have already learned. If you ask me what I had for breakfast this morning, I will tell you I had bacon and eggs. If you were to ask how I know that, I would say that I remember it. Suppose you were to then ask, "But how do you know that your memory is reliable?" I might think about that for a minute and say, "I don't know how I know that my memory is reliable, but I have no reason to question it. It has done a pretty good job so far, and, unless you can give me a reason (called a defeater) for questioning my memory, I think I am warranted in depending on it." The externalist would challenge the internalist to come up with some means for testing to see if our memories are reliable. Externalism would say that I am not obligated to justify that my memories are reliable. Just because I do not have justification in the form of evidence or reasons does not mean that I am irrational in holding that my memories are reliable, and in the absence of defeaters I am warranted in holding to my memories as reliable.[6]

To illustrate externalism, reconsider Shelley's belief (D) that God exists. Internalists claim that Shelley is not justified in believing (D) because she did not have epistemic access to the reasons and evidence that support this belief. But, according to externalism, Shelley's lack of reasons and support do not necessarily render (D) an irrational belief. They contend that all people—no matter what their occupation or religious beliefs might be—believe some things that they do not have internalist justification for, like their memories being reliable. Nevertheless,

---

[5]Alvin Plantinga, *Warrant: The Current Debate* (New York: Oxford University Press, 1993), 6.
[6]One might ask what such a defeater would look like. If someone were to point out that I had recently taken some drugs that tend to affect my memory, then that would constitute a defeater to my claim that my memory is reliable and I would have to doubt it. But in absence of such a defeater or one like it, I am justified in claiming my memory is reliable.

this does not necessarily mean that they are irrational for holding these beliefs. Most people, for example, believe something like (E)—our senses give us good and reliable information about the world. Yet, unless they have taken a course in epistemology, they have probably never considered the reasons why they hold this belief to be true. In this case, they believe (E) but do not have epistemic access to the reasons and arguments that support (E). Do we consider the vast majority of people on earth to be irrational or unjustified in their belief that (E) is true? No! (E) is a reasonable belief that virtually all human beings affirm. They are rational and justified in believing (E), even if they cannot give the reasons why they think (E) is true. Many externalists believe that Shelly may be warranted in believing in God even if she cannot offer specific reasons for her belief.

One popular and important version of externalism is known as *reliabilism*. This position states that a person can be reasonable and rational in her beliefs even if she does not have cognitive access to the reasons and evidence that support her beliefs, as long as her beliefs have been formed in a reliable fashion. In other words, rational beliefs do not necessarily require evidential support, as long as the cognitive process in forming the belief functioned reliably. As long as a person is in the right frame of mind while considering a belief, is informed by appropriate cognitive processes (memory, sense input, rational capacities) and there are no good reasons to reject the given belief, then the person who forms the belief in a reliable way is considered to be rational in holding that belief. The person does not even need to be aware that his or her cognitive processes are functioning reliably, just as long as they are.

For example, suppose I look out my window and observe my neighbor mowing his lawn. I form the belief that John has decided to mow his lawn today. Do I need to offer a justification for that belief? The externalist would say that as long as I am in the right state of mind (I have not taken any mind-altering drugs) and my cognitive process has formed a belief in a reliable way, then I am warranted in holding the belief. I do not need any further evidence or reasons to justify my belief. I do not even have to be aware that my visual senses are functioning properly. As long as they are, I am rational in believing that I know John is mowing his yard. We can imagine all kinds of other scenarios where a person may or may not have cognitive access to the reasons for the belief but still forms his belief in a reliable way. Reliabilism approaches the issue of justification in an externalist fashion.

Internalists have a number of criticisms of externalism, the most prominent being the lack of any sense of responsibility toward one's epistemic duties. Internalists have a strong sense that we have an obligation to make sure that we have good reasons to hold the beliefs we do. They believe that externalism tends to shirk this duty. Externalists' main criticism of internalism is that we do not normally form our beliefs by going through some sort of extended process of internally reflecting on reasons and evidence. They would say most of our beliefs are formed in us rather than our intentionally forming them. As we have seen, they would also argue many of our beliefs cannot be justified in the traditional sense of the word. After all, they might say, how do I *prove* my senses are giving me reliable information about the outside world?

Thus, internalists and externalists take a different view on the need for evidence and good reasons to support our beliefs. Internalists think that for our beliefs to be justified, we must have evidence for them. Externalists, by contrast, think that we do not have to access the reasons and evidence that support many of our beliefs to be counted as rational. These are the basic ideas of internalism and externalism. There is one more area we need to investigate concerning the question of justification: How are our beliefs structured?

How Is Justification Structured?

When we discuss the relationship between our beliefs, we are talking about our noetic structure.[7] Although some of our beliefs are unrelated to each other, most are related together in systems of justification. They justify one another. For example, I believe that Abraham Lincoln was president during the Civil War. If I am asked why I believe that, I justify it by appealing to history books, which are usually reliable. If I am asked why I believe history books are usually reliable, I reply that they are

---

[7]From *noeo*, the Greek term for thinking or understanding.

written by experts. If I am asked why I should trust experts, I reply we trust them because they have done the research and have the experience behind them. Each belief I hold is justified by another belief. In other words, most of our beliefs are formed in an epistemic chain: We believe proposition P because of proposition Q, and we believe proposition Q because of proposition R. Now, what is the nature of that chain? The nature of the chain depends on exactly how those beliefs are related. In general, there are two main theories of how beliefs relate: foundationalism and coherentism.

Foundationalism. Foundationalism suggests that there are two different kinds of beliefs: basic and non-basic. A basic belief is a foundational belief that does not require argumentation or empirical data to support it. Rather, basic beliefs are those which are so deeply rooted in common sense and so necessary for our thinking that they are given foundational status. We accept these beliefs as being basic, depending on nothing else for their justification. Basic beliefs serve as the foundations for our thinking and knowing. An example of this kind of belief might be something like "I exist" or "Bachelors are unmarried." A non-basic belief, by contrast, is a belief that is not so immediately obvious and rooted in common sense. These beliefs depend on other beliefs or other information for their intellectual support. An example of this kind of belief might be something like "Lincoln was the sixteenth president of the United States" or "The chemical composition of water is H_2O." Foundationalists claim that basic beliefs serve as the epistemic foundations for our believing and knowing, and non-basic beliefs must ultimately be supported by and built on basic beliefs. Accepting these kinds of beliefs prevents us from falling into an infinite epistemic regress in which we constantly have to go back to look for justification for the belief that justifies the first belief. By affirming that some beliefs are basic and require no other justification, we find an epistemic stopping point that allows us to build a system of knowledge. Foundationalism can be illustrated with a pyramid (see fig. 7.1).

Belief P is supported by a more foundational belief, Q, and Q is supported by an even more foundational belief, R. As we continue to justify our beliefs, we ultimately reach the bottom of the pyramid, a basic belief. Basic beliefs are foundational beliefs needing no justification; they are self-justifying. Philosophers have sometimes referred to them as first principles.

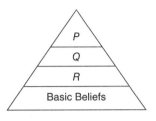

Figure 7.1. Foundationalism

Foundationalism comes in two forms: strong foundationalism and modest foundationalism.[8] What distinguish the two versions are (1) criteria a belief has to meet to be considered a properly basic belief and (2) the basing relation. The basing relation has to do with the nature of the relationship between basic beliefs and all the other beliefs above them. How strong is that relationship? Strong foundationalism takes a very restrictive view on what qualifies as a basic belief. According to Ronald Nash, classical foundationalism considers only three kinds of beliefs to be properly basic. These include beliefs which are (1) evidence of the senses, (2) self-evident and (3) incorrigible.[9] Here, a belief that is evidence of the senses—"the plane just landed"—can be counted as a basic belief because we almost always trust the information presented to us by our senses. Self-evident beliefs—"a bachelor is unmarried"—are those whose truths are obvious on first reflection. Incorrigible beliefs— the T-shirt appears blue to me—are beliefs that, given their nature, cannot be doubted. After all, no one can know any better than I how the T-shirt appears to me.[10] These are the three criteria for a basic belief according to classical foundationalism. The basing relation for classical foundationalism is that a belief can be justified only if it is either a basic belief or, as a non-basic belief, is deductively guaranteed by a basic

---

[8]Both versions are referred to by a number of names.
[9]Ronald Nash, *Faith and Reason* (Grand Rapids: Zondervan, 1988), 82.
[10]I might be wrong about what color the T-shirt is, but it is not possible for me to be wrong about how it appears to me.

belief. So consider again Shelley's belief in (D)—God exists. According to most classical foundationalists, (D) would not be counted as a basic belief. Therefore, in order for Shelley to be justified in believing (D), she must make sure that (D) is at least supported by or founded ultimately on some other basic belief. If she cannot do this, then Shelley is unjustified in believing (D).

Despite whatever influence this position had in the past, most epistemologists today think that it has significant problems. For example, Nash believes that this kind of foundationalism cannot pass its own test of rationality. He says:

> As we all remember . . . [strong] foundationalism advances the thesis that properly *basic beliefs must be evident to the senses, self-evident, or incorrigible*. It is interesting to observe what happens when one asks the narrow foundationalist whether his thesis is evident to the senses, self-evident, or incorrigible or based on propositions that are true.[11]

As Nash points out, the belief that "basic beliefs must be evident to the senses, self-evident, or incorrigible" is not itself a basic belief. Therefore, it is hard to see that this system is successful in justifying non-basic beliefs. Others, like W. Jay Wood, have noted that strong foundationalism does not sufficiently end the problem of epistemic regress. He says, "Any acceptance of supposedly pure and certain basic beliefs in fact makes use of various background assumptions or information that compromises their certainty and undermines their 'basicality.'"[12] In other words, Wood believes that even basic beliefs assume certain things that may or may not be reasonable to assume and, therefore, cannot be the solid epistemological foundations that justify our beliefs. Because of concerns like these, the vast majority of philosophers and epistemologists have moved away from strong foundationalism.

Although strong foundationalism has fallen on hard times, many philosophers have looked favorably on modest foundationalism. Like strong foundationalism, modest foundationalism maintains the distinction between basic and non-basic beliefs, as well as the idea that non-basic be-

---

[11]Ibid., 86, emphasis original.
[12]W. Jay Wood, *Epistemology: Becoming Intellectually Virtuous* (Downers Grove, IL: InterVarsity Press, 1998), 88.

liefs are justified by basic beliefs. There are, however, two important differences between modest foundationalism and strong foundationalism. First, modest foundationalists argue that strong foundationalism's criteria for basic beliefs are far too narrow. They contend for a much broader and inclusive set of basic beliefs. Like the strong foundationalists, they keep the self-evidential. However, rather than saying a belief is incorrigible (it is impossible for me to be wrong about it), modest foundationalists would say a belief is indefeasible. When we say a belief is indefeasible, we mean that we are justified in believing it because there are no defeaters or little likelihood of defeaters (defeaters are always possible, but requiring the "impossibility of defeaters" is too high a standard). Finally, the "evident to the senses" criterion is replaced with "prima facie justified." Prima facie means "at face value." The moderate foundationalist recognizes that, while it is possible that my senses could be wrong, I can take them prima facie as accurate in light of the experience I have had with them in the past and, again, in the absence of any reason why I should doubt them.

Second, modest foundationalism is a favorite of many externalists like Plantinga. Plantinga and those who follow him have been especially concerned with defending theists against the charge of irrationality for believing in God. Specifically, critics of theism charge that it is irrational to believe in God without evidence and good reasons. And because many believers are not equipped do this, critics consider them irrational. Building on the epistemological insights of some Reformed thinkers, Plantinga develops a view known as Reformed epistemology. He defends theism by rejecting strong foundationalism and developing modest foundationalism. From an externalist perspective, Plantinga suggests that it is reasonable for persons to believe in God without having evidences and arguments to justify their belief. He appeals to the concept of the *sensus divinitatis*, or "sense of God," as warrant for such a belief. Like our physical senses, the *sensus divinitatis* perceives God directly and therefore is a basic belief.

An example will illustrate the difference between classical and modest foundationalism on the question of God's existence: Shelley's belief (D)— God exists. According to internalism, Shelley is unjustified in this belief because she cannot provide reasons and evidence for it. According to classical foundationalism, (D) is a non-basic belief which must be supported by basic beliefs if Shelley is to be justified in believing it. In either case, internalists in general, and classical foundationalists in particular, believe that Shelley needs some kind of evidence or reasons for believing (D). Externalists and modest foundationalists do not believe that Shelley is required to offer reasons and evidence in support of (D) before she is justified in believing it. They arrived at this conclusion, however, by readjusting the criteria for basic beliefs. Again, strong foundationalists believe that a belief is basic if it is (1) evidence of the senses, (2) self-evident or (3) incorrigible. And because Shelley's belief in (D) could be categorized as neither (1), (2) nor (3), it must not be a basic belief according to classical foundationalism. Modest foundationalists allow for other criteria, including the possibility of a *sensus divinitatis*. If they are right, then Shelley is not required to produce evidence or reasons in favor of (D) before she can be considered rational in holding this belief. She may not even be aware of employing the *sensus divinitatis*. As long as it is functioning, she is warranted in her belief in God.

Not everyone is convinced that the modest foundationalists' attempt to make (D) a basic belief is legitimate. In fact, many have noted that this seems to be arbitrary and ad hoc, opening the door for people to insert any belief whatsoever as a basic belief which needs no justification.

Coherentism. We were earlier introduced to coherentism in chapter 4, when we were dealing with the nature of truth. There we saw that coherentism considers true statements to be those which cohere with everything else a person claims to know. If the statement is consistent with other statements that are held to be true by a particular person, then coherentists consider such statements to be true. By contrast, if the statement is inconsistent with other beliefs, then it is rejected as false belief. That was dealing with coherentism as a theory of truth. For our present discussion, however, we are not considering definitions for truth. Rather, we are dealing with the issue of justification. Here the concern is not whether or not a particular statement or idea is true. Instead, the question here is whether or not a person is justified in holding to a particular belief.

For coherentism, a person would be considered justified in holding a particular belief if that belief is consistent with everything else the person believes to be true. Here, that person believes one thing on the basis of its relationship to other ideas. Where a pyramid illustrated foundationalism, coherentism has often been pictured as a spider's web (see fig. 7.2).

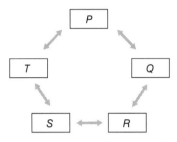

Figure 7.2. Coherentism

P is justified because it coheres with *Q*, and *Q* is justified because it coheres with *R* and *R* with *S* and so forth all around the web of beliefs. Notice that no belief is more basic than any other. There are no basic beliefs in coherentism. Each belief is supported by the beliefs around it. For example, consider your friend Charlene, who believes (F)—strawberries have a fruity taste. Now suppose also that Charlene has never tasted a strawberry. She has, however, (1) tasted many other fruits that are similar to strawberries and knows from this experience that all these fruits taste fruity. Furthermore, she also knows that (2) strawberries belong to the same general category as fruit. Based on all of this, Charlene comes to believe (F). In this example, Charlene has reason for believing (F). These reasons might not prove that (F) is true, but they would justify why Charlene believes (F). In fact, if Charlene were asked why it is that she believes (F), she can surely give two reasons: (1) that she has tasted other fruits and (2) that strawberries belong to the same category of being fruit. Charlene bases her belief on other beliefs that she holds and is able to explain the consistency of these two ideas as the justification of her belief in (F). Charlene's use of coherence functions in an internalist fashion.

A number of criticisms have been raised concerning coherentism as a way of structuring our beliefs. First, there is the problem of circularity. When you look at the diagram of a web, you can see that there is an issue of circularity. How do I justify my belief in *P*? It coheres with *Q*. How do I justify my belief in *Q*? It coheres with *R*. How do I justify my belief in *R*? It coheres with *S* and then *T* and then *P*. But it seems that we are going in a large circle here. A circular argument means there is no ultimate justification independent of the system we have. We cannot break free of the circle.

The second problem is that of isolation: Coherentism isolates my beliefs from the external world. What is real does not matter; as long as a belief coheres in the system, it is justifiable. But I want more than that. I want to know if my beliefs about the real world are true, and therefore I want a system of justification that gets me that. This can be seen by the example of Christopher Columbus. Columbus believed that he had found a new path to the Indies. In fact, he died believing that he had found that. According to coherence, he was justified in believing that. Why? Because it cohered with all his other beliefs: his maps, his assumptions about astronomy and his other assumptions about the world. And yet he was wrong in holding that he had discovered a new path to the Indies. His belief cohered with his system, but it had nothing to do with reality. We want our system of justification to talk about reality. Coherentism does not do that. Also, other questions are raised by this problem. How does one get the system started? How do I justify the first belief? I need a system of other beliefs in which it will cohere—but I do not have that yet.

A third problem is the problem of plurality: It is possible to have two coherent systems that are logically incompatible. How do I judge between them? How do I decide which system is the right one when the only way I can justify my belief is by appealing to a system? I need to step outside the system in order to judge them. But step into what? Another system? How do I know it is right? Again, we have a bit of an infinite egress here.

CAN WE FIND A BALANCED APPROACH?

So, what should we make of all this? Should we be internalists or externalists about justification? Do we need cognitive access to evidence and good reasons for what we believe in order to be counted as rational? By many accounts, the debate between these two positions has come to a stalemate. It seems as though each position is right about certain things and wrong about others. Perhaps we can find a more balanced approach that brings these two positions together. Part of this is in recognizing that we have two different kinds of beliefs. Internalists claim that we are not rational or justified in believing things without cognitive access to the reasons and evidence that support our belief. Surely there are many things that we believe for which it would be wise and desirable to have justification. This is especially true when we consider the big questions about life: Does God exist? Do I have a soul? Is there such a thing as right and wrong? These are the kinds of questions that we should at some point do more than simply believe. Yet, don't most of us come to hold these beliefs without reasons and evidence when we first believe, and isn't this normal? As human beings, don't we usually embrace some beliefs for which we do not immediately have reasons for holding? Externalists, by contrast, claim that we need not have such cognitive access in order to be rational about at least some of our beliefs: the reliability of our memories and senses. Also, when children form beliefs about almost everything, they do not normally have internalist justification for those beliefs. They see something and then believe. Admittedly, adults do this less often, but they do it nonetheless. If internalism is true, then all of this is foolishness.

Clearly then, there are times when it is critical for us to have cognitive access to the reasons and evidence for our beliefs and times when it may not be essential for us to have such evidence. But how do we determine when it is and is not necessary to have these reasons? What if we made a distinction between initial belief and continued belief? The actual beliefs held in initial and continued belief would be the same. In other words, if Shelley's belief in God, (D), is what is in question, then the belief itself does not change over time for Shelley. What is different about these two moments of belief, however, are the reasons that Shelley holds it. Reformed epistemologists, for example, are externalists about belief in God. That is, they argue that it is not irrational for Shelley to believe (D) even though she does not have cognitive access to good reasons or evidence that supports (D). If we make a distinction between initial belief and continued belief, it would seem reasonable to agree with Reformed epistemology about Shelley's initial belief in God. That is, Shelley comes to believe in God, but she cannot explain why. This does not mean that she is irrational in holding to this belief. People form beliefs about all sorts of things on a regular basis, and this is quite normal. People are not irrational for holding these beliefs initially. This is how the human mind works.

But suppose that twenty-five years go by and Shelley has continued to believe in God's existence. Her new friends ask her the same question once asked by her old friends: "Shelley, why do you believe that God exists?" While we might not be comfortable taking a hard-line internalist position about Shelley's continued belief, we would have to say that it would almost be epistemologically and spiritually unhealthy if she can give no better reason twenty-five years later to this simple question. So, what are we saying? We are saying that it is normal and acceptable that people might initially accept something as true even if they do not currently possess good reasons or evidence for this. But, when it comes to the big questions of our life, we should want to know a little bit more about this as we go along. Questions about God, surviving death and morality are too big to leave untouched over the course of our life. It is understandable and even acceptable that Shelley would not think much about her reasons for thinking about God's existence at the beginning of her spiritual journey. But as she grows in her faith and her overall intellectual maturity, these kinds of questions should receive some attention. We might say that good reasons and evidence are not necessary at the outset of these kinds of beliefs, but they become much more important as we progress in our intellectual journey. The more important a belief is to us, the more we will want at some point to pay attention to the justification of those beliefs.

Conclusion

In this chapter we have considered several important questions that pertain to the issue of justification. In particular, we have given special attention to the debate between internalism and externalism. In chapter 8, we look at virtue epistemology. There, we will describe an approach to knowledge that many believe holds promise for helping us assure true belief.

Discussion Questions

1. What do epistemologists mean when they say that a belief is justified?

2. Do we need justification for our beliefs? Why or why not?

3. What is the difference between internalism and externalism?

4. What is strong foundationalism, and how does it structure justification?

5. How does coherentism differ from foundationalism?

8

What Is Virtue Epistemology?

NOW THAT WE HAVE CONSIDERED THE ISSUES of justification and perception, we can move on to consider one of the more important developments in contemporary epistemology. Recently, a number of epistemologists have begun exploring intellectual virtues and how they might inform our approach to epistemology. These virtue epistemologists emphasize that our ability to find the truth depends in large part on the proper development and use of our intellectual virtues.

In this chapter we explore what it means to be intellectually virtuous and how this might offer a fruitful way of pursuing knowledge and finding confidence in what we believe. To do this, we will first consider the concepts of virtue and vice and what we normally mean by such terms. Second, we will note that, though normally applied to ethical discussions, the concepts of virtue and vice can also be applied to our intellectual pursuits. Third, we will consider some of the so-called intellectual virtues to see how they function in an epistemological context. And finally, we will consider how such intellectual virtues help us handle important epistemological issues.

WHAT ARE VIRTUES AND VICES?

What comes to mind when we hear the words *virtue* and *vice*? In all likelihood, we immediately begin thinking about ethics and morality. After all, it was Plato and Aristotle who had much to say about virtue, and they both developed this concept within the context of ethical and moral discussions. In the *Republic*, for example, Plato is interested in determining what justice is and why it is important for individuals and for society. Among other things, he notes that justice is a kind of virtue, along with wisdom, courage and moderation. But what, according to Plato, is a virtue? He says that virtue is "a kind of health, fine condition, and well-being of the soul," while its opposite—vice—can be understood as "disease, shameful condition, and weakness."[1] In his mind, virtues are those qualities of being that promote well-being or excellence in a person, while vices make one corrupt and unhealthy. Though he shares this understanding of virtue and vice, Aristotle offers a much more developed account of virtue as he outlines his ethical system. To understand Aristotle, we must consider his notion of happiness—*eudaimonia*. This understanding of happiness differs significantly from hedonistic notions of happiness, where pleasure and physical indulgence come to mind. In Aristotle's understanding, happiness is a sort of well-being or excellence of the soul that is "in keeping with virtue."[2] In other words, like Plato, Aristotle thought that virtues promote well-being and excellence in a particular person. But Aristotle has much more to say about this. What is unique in his account is the way he distinguishes virtue from vice. He says that virtue is the "mean between two vices, one of excess and one of deficiency."[3] That is, a virtue is a quality, or characteristic, of a person that is situated between two opposite vices.

Take, for example, the opposite vices of cowardice and rashness. The first—cowardice—is a vice of deficiency and signifies a quality in a person who is constantly afraid of danger and is thus unwilling to face difficulty for the sake of the good. The second vice—rashness—is a vice of excess and signifies a quality in a person who is too bold and brazen in the face of danger and is constantly ready to fight, even when it might be unwise to do so. In contrast to these two vices of deficiency and excess, Aristotle found the virtue of courage. Aristotle defines virtue as a middle quality or characteristic—or golden mean—that promotes well-being in those who possess it. As he explains, to be virtuous, a person cannot

---

[1]Plato, *Republic*, in *Plato: Complete Works*, ed. John M. Cooper (Indianapolis: Hackett, 1997), 444e.
[2]Aristotle, *Nicomachean Ethics* (Indianapolis: Hackett, 1999), 1099b.
[3]Ibid., 1107a.

be characterized by the vices but must instead be characterized by qualities that lead to well-being (see fig. 8.1 for a diagram of his view).

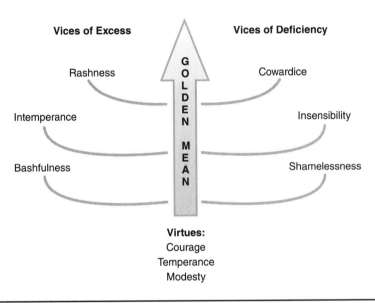

*Eudaimonia—*Happiness

Vices of Excess   **Vices of Deficiency**

Rashness   Cowardice

Intemperance   Insensibility

Bashfulness   Shamelessness

GOLDEN MEAN

Virtues:
Courage
Temperance
Modesty

Figure 8.1. Aristotle on Virtue

There is one other important point that we need to make about Plato's and Aristotle's understanding of virtue before moving forward. Aristotle, for example, has much to say about how a person comes to possess these virtues. As he makes clear, they are not in us by nature but are developed in us as we practice the right kinds of habits. Educating a person correctly is vital, and the earlier this can start the better. He says, "That is why we need to have had the appropriate upbringing—right from early youth, as Plato says—to make us find enjoyment or pain in the right things."[4]

So then, the classical philosophers like Plato and Aristotle understood virtue to be some quality or characteristic of a person that promotes health, well-being or excellence. And they argued that a person acquires virtues through proper education, practice and good habits. By contrast, vices are those qualities that are destructive to a person.

---

[4]Ibid., 1105b.

WHAT ARE INTELLECTUAL VIRTUES?

So, what is an intellectual virtue? In short, it refers to certain cognitive capacities or qualities that allow a person to think well and acquire knowledge. Or, as Duncan Pritchard has said, an intellectual virtue "is a character trait which makes you better suited to gaining the truth."[5]

Discussion about virtues and vices seems to be natural when it takes place within the context of ethics and morality. But for many people, the idea of there being such a thing as an intellectual virtue is rather odd or unexpected. Yet, despite how unusual it might seem to think this way, the concept of an intellectual virtue is as old as philosophy itself—dating once again as far back as Aristotle. In fact, at the beginning of Aristotle's consideration of virtue, he quickly distinguishes two kinds: moral and intellectual. He says, "Virtue, then, is of two sorts, virtue of thought and virtue of character."[6] Like a moral virtue, an intellectual virtue is something that confers excellence on a person's intellectual processes. These intellectual virtues include craft or art (ability to reason about production), science (the ability to deduce truth from things that are necessary), prudence (the ability to choose rationally about good and bad), wisdom (knowing how to properly apply our knowledge) and understanding (ability to apprehend the fundamental nature of reality).[7] What these abilities help us to do, according to Aristotle, is grasp the truth and attain knowledge.

We should note that those who have discussed intellectual virtues are normally careful to point out that intellectual virtues are closely related to their moral counterparts. In other words, intellectual virtues are normally thought of as being similar and closely related to moral virtues. Thomas Aquinas is a case in point. He describes intellectual virtues as a kind of cognitive capacity that "perfects man's speculative or practical intellect in order that his deed may be good."[8] In other words, in order to do well, one must first think well. But, as Aquinas and others like him would affirm, thinking well requires one to be guided by intellectual

---

[5]Duncan Pritchard, *What Is This Thing Called Knowledge?* (New York: Routledge, 2006), 58.
[6]Aristotle, *Nichomachean Ethics*, book 2, chap. 1.
[7]Ibid., 1139b15.
[8]Thomas Aquinas, *The Summa Theologica*, trans. Fathers of the English Dominican Province (Notre Dame, IN: Christian Classics, 1948), 2.58.3.

virtues. In his view, true well-being and goodness in a person require both moral and intellectual virtues to work in unison. He says, "Accordingly, for a man to do a good deed, it is requisite not only that his reason be well disposed by means of a habit of intellectual virtue; but also that his appetite be well disposed by means of a habit of moral virtue."[9]

More recently, contemporary philosophers have also been careful to note the relationship of intellectual virtues to moral virtues. W. Jay Wood, for example, has argued that intellectual virtues parallel moral virtues in at least five different ways. First, he suggests that like moral virtues, intellectual virtues are cultivated by a "developmental process extending though a lifetime." In other words, these are not like skills that we can quickly acquire. They take time and maturity along the course of our life. Second, growth in moral and intellectual virtue "is not automatic." Just because someone gets older does not necessarily mean that the person becomes morally or intellectually virtuous. Third, both moral and intellectual virtues are best developed in the context of a community, as opposed to personal isolation. Fourth, for both moral and intellectual virtues, when we have acquired a virtue, we must work to prevent regression into a vice. Fifth, "growing in intellectual virtue requires that we grow in moral virtues, and vice versa."[10]

Thus, virtue epistemologists note the similarity between intellectual and moral virtues but argue that the intellectual virtues have been underemphasized, especially in the context of epistemology. What they seek to do is develop their epistemology around these kinds of virtues. By doing so, they contend that many of the traditional problems in epistemology can be overcome and genuine progress can be made. More will be said shortly about how this kind of approach to epistemology might be helpful. Before we do this, however, let us note the kinds of intellectual virtues that might help us in our epistemological considerations. Different epistemologists offer different lists of which intellectual virtues are most important. Some that are most common are studiousness, humility, honesty, autonomy, courage, firmness, generosity and prudence. We will

---

[9]Ibid., 2.58.2.
[10]W. Jay Wood, *Epistemology: Becoming Intellectually Virtuous* (Downers Grove, IL: InterVarsity Press, 1998), 20-21.

say more about some of these later, but for now we turn to consider how these virtues can aid us epistemologically.

HOW DOES VIRTUE EPISTEMOLOGY WORK?

Virtue epistemology emphasizes the value of intellectual virtues in our pursuit of knowledge and justification. Garrett DeWeese notes that the "basic idea of virtue epistemology is that if a person faithfully employs certain intellectual virtues, the person's resultant noetic structure will be proper; that is, it will contain (mostly) true beliefs."[11] Robert C. Roberts and W. Jay Wood note, "Philosophical reflection about the intellectual virtues is still in its infancy, but we think it holds enormous promise for the recovery of epistemology as a philosophical discipline with broad human importance."[12] Elsewhere Wood puts the importance of these virtues even more strongly. He says, "Our careers as cognitive agents, as persons concerned to lay hold of the truth and pursue other important intellectual goals, will in large measure succeed or fail as we cultivate our intellectual virtues."[13] Virtue epistemology tries to do epistemology by placing intellectual virtues at the center of the enterprise.

But how do the various intellectual virtues help us achieve our epistemological goals? Again, there are various lists of intellectual virtues offered by different virtue epistemologists, but the list we mentioned a moment ago will help us to understand how this works. Consider the following intellectual virtues: studiousness, humility, honesty, autonomy, courage, firmness, generosity and prudence.

Studiousness. What does it mean to be studious, and how does this help us epistemologically? Once again, Wood offers us some helpful insights as we think through these issues. He notes the kinds of motives present within a studious person's pursuit of knowledge. He says, "Like so much of the virtuous life, seeking truth appropriately is a matter of seeking it in the right way for the right reason, using the right methods

[11]Garrett J. DeWeese, *Doing Philosophy as a Christian* (Downers Grove, IL: InterVarsity Press, 2011), 172.
[12]Robert C. Roberts and W. Jay Wood, *Intellectual Virtues: An Essay in Regulative Epistemology* (New York: Oxford University Press, 2010), 6.
[13]Wood, *Epistemology*, 16.

and for the right purposes."[14] In other words, a studious person will be one who greatly desires knowledge but will go about getting that knowledge and using that knowledge in a virtuous fashion. She will not stoop to doing immoral things to gain that knowledge and will not misuse that knowledge once she has it. Rather, she will seek knowledge for her own well-being and the well-being of others.

Perhaps some illustrations will help. Consider a person who has a raging desire to learn about the stock market. She buys every book she can find, attends all the seminars available and even enrolls in the local university's business school to learn all she can. So far, nothing sounds problematic. But suppose that her pursuits are motivated by an unhealthy greed for money and fame. In this case, her concern will not be with the help of her own soul or with the well-being of other people around her. Those infected with this kind of greed often corrupt themselves and bring much harm to others around them. These kinds of vices not only harm other people but also often cloud our ability to see things as they really are. Thus, the studious person is one whose hunger for knowledge is grounded in the right kinds of motives and desires for well-being.

Humility. What about the epistemic virtue of humility? Most of us know what it means for a person to be humble. We typically refer to someone as humble when he is not self-promoting or boastful about his accomplishments but instead offers a modest appraisal of himself when asked by someone else. Epistemic humility is related to this but is applied specifically to the way humility might function in our pursuit of knowledge. When this is done, it is quite easy to see how humility is an intellectual virtue. After all, many of the problems we face as those seeking truth and knowledge come from overstatement and exaggeration.

Some philosophers, like Linda Trinkaus Zagzebski, have applied Aristotle's idea on the golden mean—virtue as the mean between two opposing vices—to the issue of humility. She suggests that epistemic humility "could reasonably be interpreted as a mean between the tendency to grandiosity and the tendency to a diminished sense of her own

---

[14]Ibid., 57.

ability."[15] Consider someone very prideful about her ability to reason and argue. Such a person normally makes bold dogmatic statements about things that require a bit more caution and reservation. Yet, because she thinks so highly of herself intellectually, she is prone to make grandiose claims and affirmations. This is detrimental to her and those she influences because it creates an unwarranted sense of assurance about things that could be questionable. When this happens, we tend to shut off further conversation and limit our ability to gain greater knowledge. Of course, the opposite is also a concern. Some people are so intimidated by intellectual questions that they give up before they have even started. They immediately assume that they are not smart enough to wrestle with difficult questions and thus never pursue knowledge the way they should. By contrast, intellectually virtuous persons will admit their intellectual weaknesses and limitations but will not let these limitations keep them from pursuing the knowledge that is necessary for life. This kind of humility seeks to know things but admits what it does not or cannot know.

Roberts and Wood suggest that humility is best represented by contrasting it to vanity and arrogance.[16] Consider the way vanity plays a part in our lives. Desiring the attention and praise of others, we go to great lengths to make this happen. Unfortunately, we also do this with our intellectual lives. That is, some seek after knowledge and degrees so that others will notice them or esteem them highly. Because the praise of a peer is what is most important, this person will be quick to give the impression of being knowledgeable, when in fact there could be huge pockets of ignorance. Arrogance also limits our ability because it causes us to listen less to others who have something legitimate to say. In either case, failure to be humble stifles intellectual progress.

Honesty. A little reflection will also show why intellectual honesty is helpful for us epistemologically. Just as we are sometimes prone to exaggerate the truth, we are also at times tempted to lie about things or present the facts in a biased way. Needless to say, this is harmful to our pursuit for knowledge. Consider an example from the legal profession.

---

[15]Linda Trinkaus Zagzebski, *Virtues of the Mind: An Inquiry into the Nature of Virtue and the Ethical Foundations of Knowledge* (New York: Cambridge University Press, 1998), 220.
[16]Roberts and Wood, *Intellectual Virtues*, 237-50.

When someone is murdered in the United States, a criminal investigation takes place in which police and detectives explore the crime scene and all the available evidence to try and determine who the killer might be. They are often able to find the person and apply the appropriate measure of justice. However, they are not always able to find the guilty person, so the killer goes free. What is even more problematic is when prosecutors charge and convict the wrong person for such crimes.

With the advent of DNA testing, many of these cases have come to the public's attention in recent years. There are numerous examples that could be considered here, but in most cases, a person is wrongly convicted of murder and then, after spending years or even decades in prison or on death row, is acquitted by new DNA tests that prove that person's innocence. This by itself is alarming and problematic. To make matters worse, however, there are also occasions where, during the original murder trial, the prosecution withholds key evidence that could have proven the innocence of the defendant from the start. Yet, because this evidence is withheld from the jury, the jury finds the defendant guilty of a crime that he or she did not commit. In these cases, the killer goes free and an innocent person loses years of his or her life, or maybe even life itself.

We can give examples of other cases where people lie, exaggerate or withhold evidence. Consider what two siblings do when they break their mother's favorite lamp and then report what happened to their parents. Each child presents what happened in a lopsided way that makes him look innocent and his sibling look guilty. Or, consider salespeople who are sometimes prone to lie about the value of a product to a potential customer. And of course, we could cite numerous examples of the way that politicians stretch the truth or present half facts to their voters. In all these cases, whether you are a juror, parent, customer or voter, it is often extremely difficult to find what is true. These are all problems that arise from other people being dishonest with us. But similar problems might also arise when we are dishonest with ourselves. Thus, honesty is a sort of intellectual virtue that counters these problems and makes the acquisition of knowledge much easier. Those who are governed by it will have more epistemic success than those who are not.

Courage. We can say something similar about those who are epistemically courageous. At first, this kind of idea might seem a bit odd. But consider the social pressure that people experience from the groups that they belong to about the beliefs that they hold. In many cases, people can be condemned or rejected by their ideological or social group when their beliefs begin to change. Yet, intellectual courage allows people to endure such oppositions from those close to them as they explore new information and modify their beliefs accordingly. Intellectually courageous persons will not be cowards in the face of social pressure. Likewise, it will not be their goal to question every idea of their group in a brash fashion. Instead, they allow the evidence and information to guide them as they seek the truth on a given issue.

One classic example would be Copernicus and Galileo, who brought a major shift in the way we think about the arrangement of the universe. While Copernicus used mathematics, Galileo invented a telescope to look at the planets and the stars. Both men, however, argued the same point: namely, the earth is not the center of the universe. Whereas Copernicus's work was not published until right at his death, Galileo was in his prime when he developed and articulated his view. He faced considerable difficulty from the church; he was forced to recant his view and later was excommunicated from the church.

Why was intellectual courage vital for Copernicus and Galileo, and how did it make a difference? It took courage because they faced tremendous oppositions from the religious authorities of their day for saying what they said about the earth and the rest of the universe. Saying what they said could have cost them their very lives. And yet, as we look back on the history of cosmology and natural science, it was vitally important that they, or at least someone, say what they said. If they had not, then we never would have known the way the universe is structured, and science itself would have been greatly limited. Their intellectual (and moral) courage led to a whole new world of knowledge that the modern world is built on.

Carefulness. We could also say that carefulness can be counted as an intellectual virtue. Earlier we looked at the way that we draw inferences about the world in which we live and the events that take place therein.

We see something happen and then draw an inference about its meaning or cause. Fortunately, we draw inferences so often that we become quite skillful at this. Nevertheless, there are still numerous scenarios in life where we move too quickly over the information available to us and draw the wrong inference from what we see. In these cases, we need to be more careful and deliberate in the information gathering process and more attentive in the work of drawing an inference.

Consider an example from the medical profession. Studies have shown that some doctors spend very little time listening to patients about their symptoms on office visits. In some cases, it can be as little as fifteen or twenty seconds. Given the demands of their busy schedules and the fact that many patients have obvious textbook symptoms of a particular sickness, it is easy to understand why this happens so often. After listening for a brief time, the doctor comes to a diagnosis, writes a prescription and is off to the next sick patient. Most of the time, this works. Sometimes, however, the situation can be more complicated than it may first appear and a serious problem can go untreated. In these cases, catastrophic consequences follow from a failure to give careful examination to a patient's health.

Our point here is not to criticize doctors but to illustrate the danger of giving haphazard consideration to important information in our quest for truth. When we fail to be as careful as we can possibly be, or when we allow ourselves to be blinded by our preconceived notions of what is the case, we limit our ability to find the truth and secure knowledge. Carefulness, then, is that intellectual virtue that forces us to slow down, gather all the important data we have available to us, think clearly and draw a conclusion with caution. When we do this, we are in a better position to gain knowledge.

WHAT DOES VIRTUE EPISTEMOLOGY GIVE US?

Virtue epistemology attempts to emphasize the important role that intellectual virtue should play in our pursuit of knowledge. By being intellectually virtuous, we increase our ability to make discoveries, discern truth and avoid major epistemological errors. Specifically, we can identify several important contributions that this approach to epistemology makes.

First, and most obviously, this approach avoids obvious though common epistemological errors. Consider some of the examples we have noted in this chapter, such as humility, honesty and courage. As we have seen, arrogance can have some stifling effects on our ability to find the truth. Those who claim they know it all tend to ignore the contribution that others have to make about important matters. A dose of humility, however, goes a long way toward overcoming this tendency, reopening important dialogues where new insights will be gained. We have also seen how dishonesty can have catastrophic consequences for us in our quest for truth. When all relevant evidence is not considered, we can make misguided decisions on all kinds of important matters. Being intellectually and morally virtuous enough to allow all the evidence to be considered helps to avoid these kinds of problems. Intellectual courage is also important to us in our quest for knowledge and understanding. As we have seen, this kind of courage enabled some of the greatest minds to endure opposition for the sake of better understanding our physical world.

Second, this approach sets a reasonable and attainable goal for our knowledge by seeking to be intellectually virtuous instead of absolutely certain. We will consider the issue of certainty in more detail in chapter 10. But for now we note that there are many things that we cannot be certain about. Does this fact create an epistemic crisis for us? It should not. It is always possible for us to misunderstand what we see or claim to know, but it is also possible that we can prevent the mistakes that cause us to misunderstand what we see. If certainty is our goal, then our epistemic quests will be marked by continued failure. But if our goal is to be as reasonable as possible in our knowledge claims, then the intellectual virtues are a tremendous benefit for us. These virtues help us avoid errors and gain a better appreciation of what is real and true. This approach strives for being intellectually virtuous, not certain.

Finally, some philosophers have argued that virtue epistemology can help us with certain kinds of epistemological puzzles like the Gettier problem. Recall from chapter 2 that the Gettier problem suggests an inadequacy in the traditional account of knowledge: Knowledge as justified true belief (JTB). Suppose that you claim that you see your mom in a room, and she was in the room. In this case, you believe she is in the room, you have justification for believing she is in the room (you see her talking), and she really is in the room. But, as the Gettier problem would suggest, this is not knowledge, because your justification is insufficient. As it turns out, the person you saw talking (which was your justification) was your mom's identical twin sister, who was wearing the exact same clothes as your mom. But because your mom was in the room, where was she when you saw her twin? As it turns out, she was right around the corner sitting on the couch, just outside your view. Gettier suggests that because of cases like these, JTB is an inadequate account of knowledge. The problem here is the J in JTB, because your justification is insufficient.

In response, some philosophers have suggested that JTB might still work as long as the justification for a belief J is acquired in a virtuous fashion. In other words, if you have been as careful as possible in acquiring the belief that you see your mom in the room and have considered all the evidence necessary to draw that conclusion, then your JTB may very well yield knowledge. In short, some philosophers think that this approach can help us resolve some of the concerns raised by the Gettier problem.

CONCLUSION

In this chapter we have discussed intellectual virtues and how they can play into our epistemological quest in a fruitful way. Like their moral counterparts, intellectual virtues are cognitive qualities that promote excellence on us as knowers. In short, we have seen that intellectual virtues help us avoid some of the most dangerous epistemological errors that we are prone to make and help us develop good belief-forming habits.

DISCUSSION QUESTIONS

1. What is a virtue, and how does it differ from a vice?

2. What are intellectual virtues, and how do they function within epistemology?

3. What are some examples of intellectual virtues, and what epistemological advantages do they give us?

9

Do We Have Revelation?

IN THIS CHAPTER WE DEAL WITH THE ISSUE of divine revelation. This is a subject matter that is rarely addressed in other, more traditional works on epistemology. For many epistemologists, discussion on divine revelation seems to be highly speculative in nature, and thus it is avoided. But for Christians and other religious persons, this kind of question is important. Specifically, we will note why revelation is important for religious belief and what function it serves. After this, we will consider the issue of natural revelation and the prospects of doing natural theology, to see if this might offer us some information about religious matters. And finally, we will consider the prospects of Christianity's teaching that God has given us a special revelation of himself in his Son and the Bible.

As we begin, let us consider an important question: Is it really possible to know God or to know anything about God? There are two possible answers to this question. If, for example, God has not revealed himself to human beings in some way, then the answer would have to be no—we cannot have knowledge of God. If, however, God has revealed himself in some way to human beings, then the answer would be yes—it is possible to have knowledge of God. So then, the importance of divine revelation cannot be overstated for religious belief, especially from within a Christian view of God. Christianity has traditionally said that God has revealed himself in at least two ways: natural revelation and special revelation. It is important here for us to say more about each one of these so that we can later consider whether or not these give us a proper basis for divine knowledge.

Does Nature Give Us Any Knowledge of God?

Christianity affirms that God has revealed himself in two broad forms: natural (or general) revelation and special revelation. We will say more about special revelation momentarily. But for now, let us consider natural revelation. By most accounts, natural revelation refers to the knowledge or information about God that can be derived from nature—understanding nature in the broadest terms to include all of creation. Thomas Aquinas, for example, said:

> Every effect in some degree represents its cause, but diversely. For some effects represent only the causality of the cause, but not its form; as smoke represents fire. . . . Other effects represent the cause as regards the similitude of its form, as fire generated represents fire generating. . . . Therefore in rational creatures, possessing intellectual act and will, there is found the representation of the Trinity by way of image, inasmuch as there is found in them the word conceived, and the love proceeding.[1]

Even John Calvin, who felt that sin had significantly hindered our ability to properly use natural revelation, affirmed that God revealed himself in nature. He famously said:

> [God] not only sowed in men's minds that seed of religion of which we have spoken but revealed himself and daily discloses himself in the whole workmanship of the universe. As a consequence, men cannot open their eyes without being compelled to see him. . . . But upon his individual works he has engraved unmistakable marks of his glory, so clear and so prominent that even unlettered and stupid folk cannot plead the excuse of ignorance.[2]

Other examples of this can be found in the writings of Clement of Alexandria, Augustine, Boethius and Anselm. Thus, throughout the history of the church, Christians believed that God has revealed himself in the created order of the world.

But how useful is this revelation to us with regard to our knowledge of God? Can it be used to make or support theological statements about

---

[1]Thomas Aquinas, *The Summa Theologica*, trans. Fathers of the English Dominican Province (Notre Dame, IN: Christian Classics, 1948), 1.45.7.
[2]John Calvin, *Institutes of the Christian Religion*, ed. John T. McNeill, trans. Ford Lewis Battles, 2 vols. (Philadelphia: Westminster Press, 1960), 1.5.1.

God? These questions call us to make an important distinction between natural revelation and natural theology. For theologians and philosophers, natural revelation and natural theology are often thought of as being the same thing. And to be clear they are closely related to each other, as one (natural theology) depends on the other (natural revelation). But there is in fact an important difference. Whereas natural revelation refers to what God has revealed of himself, natural theology refers to our attempts to say something about God in light of what we find in nature. As such, natural revelation is something that God gives, while natural theology is something that we do.

With this distinction in mind, we might want to consider a simple question: Is natural theology a genuine possibility? In other words, is it possible to say something about God (his existence, nature, will, and so on) by considering the natural world? Historically speaking, many theologians have thought that the answer is yes—we can say something about God based on the natural world. Aquinas, for example, used reason and nature to formulate five different arguments for God's existence:

1. The argument from motion
2. The argument from causation
3. The argument from possibility and necessity
4. The argument from gradation
5. The argument from purpose[3]

William Paley (1743–1805), a pastor and theologian, is another prime example of this view. While considering a wide variety of the physical world that appears to be designed, he said, "There cannot be a design without a designer; contrivance without a contriver; order without a choice; arrangement, without any thing capable of arranging."[4] Aquinas and Paley represent just two examples of those who have thought that nature could tell us something about God. Over the last few hundred years, however, some objections have been raised to this view by phi-

---

[3]Aquinas, *Summa Theologica*, 1.2.3.
[4]William Paley, *Natural Theology*, ed. Matthew D. Eddy and David Knight (New York: Oxford University Press, 2006), 12.

losophers, scientists and theologians. Because our primary concern in this book is with philosophy, we will focus most of our attention on these philosophical objections. Nevertheless, a word is in order about the theological and scientific concerns.

Objections to natural theology. Karl Barth and many in the Reformed tradition have argued against natural revelation and natural theology, suggesting that it is dangerous for Christian thought.[5] In their mind, such practices subvert the authority of Scripture and allow theology to develop autonomously from faith in Christ. But this concern seems to be misplaced, because the Bible itself affirms God has revealed himself in nature. For example, Psalm 19:1-3 says:

> The heavens declare the glory of God;
> And the firmament shows His handiwork.
> Day unto day utters speech,
> And night unto night reveals knowledge.
> There is no speech nor language
> Where their voice is not heard.[6]

Here the psalmist affirms that God's glory and handiwork are shown throughout the universe in the unfolding of each day and each night. Moreover, he argues that this kind of revelation has gone into all places for all people to see, no matter what language they speak. The apostle Paul makes a similar point in Romans 1:18-20:

> For the wrath of God is revealed from heaven against all ungodliness and unrighteousness of men, who suppress the truth in unrighteousness, because what may be known of God is manifest in them, for God has shown it to them. For since the creation of the world His invisible attributes are clearly seen, being understood by the things that are made, even His eternal power and Godhead, so that they are without excuse.

Interestingly, Paul notes here that creation shows not only the existence of God but also his eternal power. Although this may not be enough revelation to say everything about God that a person would want

---

[5]See Emil Brunner and Karl Barth, *Natural Theology*, trans. Peter Fraenkel (Eugene, OR: Wipf & Stock, 2002).
[6]All passages are taken from the NKJV.

to say, it is enough to leave all people without excuse, according to the apostle. So then, according to the Christian Scriptures there are at least a few simple things that nature tells us about God. And if God has given this information about himself to us via natural revelation, why is it problematic to include these insights into our theological affirmation about God?

The practice of using natural theology was greatly shaken by the advent of Charles Darwin's work on evolution. In short, Darwin offered what appeared to be a workable option for the question of origins. Up until this, naturalistic explanations tended to rely on time and chance to account for the diversity of animal life. But with Darwin, the process of natural selection offered a mechanism which would account for the development of the various kinds of creatures. He says:

> As man can produce and certainly has produced a great result by his methodical and unconscious means of selection, what may not nature effect? Man can act only on external and visible characters: nature cares nothing for appearances, except in so far as they may be useful to any being. They can act on every internal organ, on every shade of constitutional difference, on the whole machinery of life.[7]

Darwin's theory was seen by many to be the end of natural theology. But more recently, the emergence of the intelligent design movement, as well as discoveries about how the universe is finely tuned, have reopened the scientific discussion on natural theology. Darwinism is no longer considered to be the great obstacle for doing natural theology that people once thought it was.

As we have noted, the philosophical objections to natural theology are our primary concern. Starting in the Enlightenment, some philosophers grew suspicious about our ability to know anything about God and the metaphysical realm by considering the physical world in which we live. In other words, they argued that nature cannot tell us anything about God and is therefore of no value to us as a form of revelation. David Hume, for example, thought that it was impossible to make theological or metaphysical statements based on what we find in the physical realm.

---

[7]Charles Darwin, *On the Origin of Species* (Cambridge, MA: Harvard University Press, 1964), 83.

In his famous *Dialogues Concerning Natural Religion*, Hume said, "We can express our adoration of him. But let us beware, lest we think, that our ideas anywise correspond to his perfections, or that his attributes have any resemblance to these qualities among men. He is infinitely superior to our limited view and comprehension."[8] In other words, Hume thought we were free to attribute praise or adoration to the one we might call God. But we could not know anything about this being—at least not on the basis of what we find here on earth. As he argued throughout the *Dialogues*, no inferences we make from the physical to the metaphysical are viable. In his mind, one of the primary weaknesses with arguments for God's existence is that their conclusions go beyond what is supported by the evidence. That is, he thought that evidence might very well show there was a cause of the world, but this evidence did not necessarily support the claim that God was the cause of the universe.

One of the strongest philosophical critics of natural theology was the eighteenth-century philosopher Immanuel Kant. For Kant, all knowledge was required to have some sort of experiential basis. As he made clear, experience and sense data are not the only components of our knowledge and cognitive processes, but knowledge is impossible without experience and sense data. He famously said:

> That all our knowledge begins with experience there can be no doubt. For how is it possible that the faculty of cognition should be awakened into exercise otherwise than by means of objects which affect our senses, and partly of themselves produce representations, partly rouse our powers of understanding and activity, to compare, to connect, or to separate these, and so to convert the raw material of our sensuous impressions into a knowledge of objects, which is called experience? In respect of time, therefore, no knowledge of ours is antecedent to experience, but begins with it.[9]

We cannot miss the significance of what Kant is saying in this quote. He believed that all of our knowledge requires some sort of experiential basis. If we do not have sense data, then we cannot have knowledge. And

---

[8]David Hume, *Dialogues Concerning Natural Religion* (London: Penguin, 1990), 53.
[9]Immanuel Kant, *Critique of Pure Reason*, trans. J. M. D. Meiklejohn (Amherst, NY: Prometheus, 1990), 1.

because we do not see, touch, taste, smell or hear God directly, Kant's model does not allow divine knowledge to come from the physical world (see fig. 9.1).

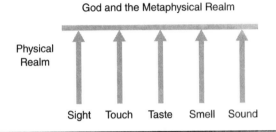

Figure 9.1. Kant's Model of Metaphysical Knowledge

Notice that there is a hard line between the physical and the metaphysical realms. Note also that each of the five senses—sight, touch, taste, smell and sound—is unable to cross the metaphysical divide. This is Kant's way of saying that we do not have access to God or metaphysical things by way of the physical world and our senses. Alister McGrath explains the significance of Kant's argument when he says, "Kant argued that God was not a noble object or phenomenon, but a transcendent reality only accessible by faith. Kant's approach thus erects a theologically impervious barrier between nature and God, preventing human inquiries into nature from reaching any meaningful conclusions concerning God."[10] Many non-Christian and Christian philosophers and theologians believe that Kant was right. So, despite the popularity of natural theology in the past, modern thinkers have been suspicious about the possibility of gaining divine knowledge from nature.

Response. What should we think about all this? Is it the case that we can learn nothing about God by considering the physical realm? Surely Hume and Kant raise some legitimate concerns, but there is reason to think that they do not successfully defeat natural theology. Let us begin with two of their concerns that are helpful. First, Hume showed that there is a tendency on the part of natural theologians to overstate their case. In some cases, for example, natural theologians argued that evi-

---

[10]Alister E. McGrath, *The Open Secret: A New Vision for Natural Theology* (Malden, MA: Blackwell, 2008), 157.

dence of design in the universe could be used as a proof for the God of Christianity. But does design in nature prove this conclusion?

Hume rejected this conclusion, and more recent versions of natural theology have been more modest in their claims. Unlike versions prior to Hume, recent arguments normally argue that the evidence points toward a creator or designer of some kind which is highly consistent with the Christian view, even if it does not prove it with absolute certainty. These revised arguments seem to be better arguments, and they bypass Hume's criticism. Moreover, these more modest versions of natural theology are more in line with older, more traditional versions espoused by theologians like Aquinas. For Aquinas, natural revelation did not give specific information about God, and thus, natural theologians should not try to be specific about God either. Instead, Aquinas limited his natural theology to say nothing more than that it points toward God's existence. He said, "To know that God exists in a general and confused way is implanted in us by nature. . . . This, however, is not to know absolutely that God exists; just as to know that someone is approaching is not the same as to know that Peter is approaching."[11] In other words, Aquinas thought that nature points to God but does not prove absolutely that he exists. Furthermore, nature does not indicate what God is like. Surely Aquinas was right about this. By looking at the specific details of nature, we do not formulate our belief in the Trinity or learn about the incarnation of Jesus Christ. Instead, we depend on the Bible to tell us about all of these things.

Second, Kant was surely right in suggesting that we do not have direct access to God with our senses. It is the case that we do not see, touch, hear, taste or smell God directly. But does this prove that the physical realm can tell us nothing about God? It does not look like it. Kant might be right in saying that we do not directly apprehend God with our senses, but must our apprehension of God be direct? What about indirect apprehension of God? In other words, what if we find evidence in nature that is best explained by God, or is at least highly consistent with the idea that God is the creator? Wouldn't this count in helping us to know something about God?

---

[11]Aquinas, *Summa Theologica*, 1.2.1.

In the last few decades, a number of scientists and philosophers have taken note of what is often called the anthropic principle, which points to examples of fine-tuning in the universe. Hugh Ross is one scientist who has done great work in this area. He argues that the anthropic principle can be seen in the universe as a whole as well as the earth itself. In various places, he has argued that there are numerous conditions of the universe that must be "just so" if there is to be any life at all.[12] Because the list grows with time, these features are not the only ones that could be listed as examples of fine-tuning in the earth and universe. Nevertheless, what is known today about the fitness of the universe for human life is enough to show that the evidence for design is tremendous. If so, then even though we might not have direct access to God with our senses, we may still indirectly perceive him through the evidence we find in nature.

Because of these considerations, many feel that it is possible to develop a modified form of natural theology. Today, advocates of natural theology are normally quick to note that scientific and philosophical reflection on nature might point us toward a particular theological conclusion but do not establish anything with absolute certainty. Furthermore, these considerations give us at most very limited insights about God. They might show, for example, that God exists and is powerful and wise but are insufficient to say everything about God that we would want to say. Without the Bible, there is little we could know about the nature of God or the specifics of Christianity. Therefore, the Bible plays an enormous role in our thinking and understanding about God. If God has not revealed himself in some special way, then our knowledge of the divine will be limited. This leads us to our second major question in this chapter: Do we have any special or specific revelation about God?

---

[12]Hugh Ross, *The Fingerprint of God*, 2nd ed. (New Kensington, PA: Whitaker House, 1989), 129-31. Some of these include (1) number of stars in the planetary system; (2) parent star birth date; (3) parent star age; (4) parent star distance from center of galaxy; (5) parent star mass; (6) parent star color; (7) surface gravity; (8) distance from parent star; (9) axial tilt; (10) rotation period; (11) gravitational interaction with a moon; (12) magnetic field; (13) thickness of crust; (14) albedo (ratio of reflected light to total amount falling on surface); (15) oxygen to nitrogen ratio in atmosphere; (16) carbon dioxide and water vapor levels in atmosphere; (17) ozone level in atmosphere; (18) atmospheric electric discharge rate; (19) oxygen quantity in atmosphere; (20) seismic activity.

Do We Have Special Revelation?

So far we have explained how it is possible to develop a limited approach to natural theology, which allows us to make some positive statements about God by considering nature. But in truth, the vast majority of what we affirm regarding God, Jesus, human beings, the world, and other important spiritual matters find their doctrinal basis in the Bible, not nature. For example, Christians believe that God is triune: one in essence and three in persons—Father, Son and Spirit. Christians also affirm that God is good, loving, wise, powerful, just and gracious. Additionally, Christians believe that God sent his Son into the world to die for the sins of humankind. These are just a few of the primary beliefs that Christians hold to be true. But where did we learn all these things? What source supplied this information to us? Was it the stars, earth or some other part of creation? Surely Christianity teaches that God has at least partially revealed himself in the created order of the world, but Christianity also admits that we are limited in what we can know about God from this kind of general or natural revelation.

As we begin our discussion about special revelation, we should note that Christianity affirms that special revelation has come in two forms: Jesus Christ incarnate and the Bible. In other words, Christians believe that we can have specific knowledge about God and salvation because Jesus became incarnate and revealed God to us and because the Bible itself is a direct word from God. But do either, or both, of these things give us revelation? As we will see, how we answer that question will depend on the reasons we might have for thinking that Christ was the Son of God. If he was the Son of God, then there seems to be ample reason for thinking that we have special revelation. However, before we can consider whether or not there is reason to think Christ is the divine Son, we must first consider what Christianity affirms about the incarnation and the Bible.

The incarnation of Jesus Christ as revelation. Christianity affirms that the Son of God became incarnate as the person Jesus Christ. Specifically, John 1:14 and John 1:18 state: "And the Word became flesh and dwelt among us, and we beheld His glory, the glory as of the only begotten of the Father, full of grace and truth. . . . No one has seen God at any time.

The only begotten Son, who is in the bosom of the Father, He has declared *Him*."

Notice here that John states that the Son (Word) came in real flesh and was beheld by people on earth. Moreover, notice that his presence on earth served as a revelation to us about God. Jesus made a similar statement in John 14:9. When asked by Philip to show him the Father, Jesus responded by saying, "Have I been with you so long, and yet you have not known Me, Philip? He who has seen Me has seen the Father." Here, Jesus suggests that he is a clear revelation of who and what God is. Some theologians (Barth, for example) have emphasized this point. He said, "Revelation in fact does not differ from the Person of Jesus Christ, and again does not differ from the reconciliation that took place in Him. To say revelation is to say, 'The Word became flesh.'"[13] Some theologians criticize Barth for underemphasizing the Bible's status as revelation, but virtually no theologian would disagree with Barth that Jesus is perhaps the best example of God revealing himself directly.

Let us consider what the implications might be if Jesus is the Son of God. If one grants that Jesus is the Son of God, then it appears that we can now begin to say and know many different things about God. To begin with, the doctrine of the Trinity starts to come into view. We also begin to have a better understanding of God's redeeming love, mercy and grace. In short, there are many different ideas about God that either emerge for the first time or find great support in the person of Jesus Christ. And so, given who Jesus is and what he does while on earth, we are able to learn something about God that we would not have otherwise been able to know. This, of course, depends on whether or not Jesus is the Son of God. If he is not, then his life does not yield valuable insights into the nature and being of God. If he is, however, this would be quite significant. We will say more about the rationale for believing that Jesus is the Son of God shortly. For now, let us turn to consider the Bible as a source of revelation.

The Bible as revelation. Christianity claims to have a unique Word from God: the Bible. In short, Christianity affirms that God has revealed

---

[13]Karl Barth, *Church Dogmatics*, trans. G. T. Thomson, vol. 1.1 (Edinburgh: T & T Clark, 1955), 368.

himself in a special way in and through the pages of Scripture. This is affirmed by numerous theologians throughout history and by the Bible itself. For example, in 2 Timothy 3:16-17, the Bible says, "All Scripture is given by inspiration of God, and is profitable for doctrine, for reproof, for correction, for instruction in righteousness, that the man of God may be complete, thoroughly equipped for every good work." Notice here that the Bible claims to be inspired by God and that it offers insights and lessons that are profitable for living the Christian life.

The Bible's status as divine revelation is important to Christians, not just because it gives them instruction in righteousness but also because of what it tells us about God. Without it, there are many different things that we could never know about God. Even Aquinas, who is widely known for his use of natural revelation and practice of natural theology, made it clear that we could never gain salvation without the witness of Christian Scripture. He said:

> I answer that, It was necessary for man's salvation that there should be a knowledge revealed by God, besides philosophical science built up by human reason. . . . But the end must first be known by men who are to direct their thoughts and actions to the end. Hence it was necessary for the salvation of man that certain truths which exceed human reason should be made known to him by divine revelation.[14]

In other words, if nothing else, the message of salvation preached and proclaimed in Christianity would not be known to us unless it was given explicitly in Scripture. But this is not all that we learn about. In Scripture we are told that God is wise, merciful, powerful, just, loving and good. If these things had not been expressed to us directly through Scripture, then we would have only hints of these kinds of things. In the Christian faith, the Bible serves as an important source of information about God.

Let us affirm that we accept the Bible as being from God and that it is, therefore, a primary source of information to us about our religious concerns. But we should want to know whether or not this is a reasonable thing for us to believe. In other words, what reasons do we have for thinking that the Bible has come from God and gives us reliable infor-

---

[14]Aquinas, *Summa Theologica*, 1.1.1.

mation? When questions like these emerge, defenders of the Bible normally do one of several things. First, they might reference various passages in the Bible, such as 2 Timothy 3:16, which explicitly affirm the Bible's status as God's Word. However, that response merely begs the question. The Bible does state that it comes from God, but this does not prove that it did. We must remember that there are a variety of different religious books that make similar or identical claims. Thus, the claim that a book is from God offers no convincing reason for thinking that it is true. Second, defenders of the Bible might also note how historically reliable the Bible is. They might say, for example, that the details given in the Old Testament and the New Testament have held up to historical scrutiny. Although this is an important point regarding the reliability and trustworthiness of the Bible, this also does not necessarily mean that the Bible did in fact come from God. After all, plenty of other documents and books are historically reliable, but this does not make them the Word of God. Third, a defender might argue that the Bible has been well-preserved since the time when its books were first written. But once again, this does not necessarily mean that the Bible came from God. We can think of many different documents that have been accurately preserved (such as the Declaration of Independence, the US Constitution or the writings of C. S. Lewis), but this does not make them God's Word.

So, what do we need in order to think that we have special revelation about God? In short, we need some reason to think that Jesus Christ was who he claimed to be: the Son of God. If he was the Son of God, then it looks like we are within our epistemic rights for seeing his life on earth and the Bible itself as sources of divine revelation. Let us consider this rationale.

Rationale. Our belief that the incarnation of Jesus Christ and the Bible give us special revelation about God depends on Jesus being the Son of God. If he was not, then neither of these tells us anything about God. If, however, he is the Son of God, then our beliefs about the incarnation and the Bible as revelation gain considerable support. We might outline our rationale in the following way.[15]

---

[15]A similar type of argument has been developed by Norman Geisler in *Christian Apologetics* (Peabody, MA: Prince Press, 2002). Our rationale is similar to his in its goal and the kinds of

1. The Gospels are good history.[16]

2. The Gospels tell us what Jesus taught.
    a. He was the divine Son of God.
    b. He would be crucified and raised again.
    c. The Old Testament is the Word of God.
    d. The apostles would be given divine guidance and remembrance.

3. The Gospels tell us about the events surrounding Jesus' death.
    a. He was crucified, dead and buried.
    b. The disciples were cowards both before and immediately after his death.
    c. His tomb was well-known and well-guarded.
    d. Three days later, the tomb was empty.
    e. Jesus reappeared to various believers and non-believers after the tomb was empty.
    f. The disciples were radically transformed after seeing Jesus alive again.

4. Jesus rose from the dead.

5. Jesus is the Son of God.

Critics will immediately notice that this rationale relies on evidence which is found in the Bible. They may be inclined to suggest that this argument begs the question as soon as this evidence is employed. Or, put another way, they might suggest it is a circular argument, because it tries to defend the Bible as God's Word while citing it to support our argument. We readily admit we rely on biblical data at this point. Yet, this does not appear to be problematic if in fact the Bible reports reliable information about the events surrounding Jesus' life and death. This is why statement (1) is important for us at this point. It has been argued by numerous scholars that the Gospels provide good history about Jesus' life and death. Gary Habermas, for example, has demonstrated that essential events of Jesus' life and death are substantiated and supported by archaeological

---

evidence considered, but it is different in structure and development. We are also indebted to our colleague Bruce Little for the many conversations we have had on this topic, which has allowed this rationale to take form.

[16]See F. F. Bruce, *The New Testament Documents: Are They Reliable?* (Grand Rapids: Eerdmans, 2003); Craig L. Blomberg, *The Historical Reliability of the Gospels* (Downers Grove, IL: InterVarsity Press, 2007).

evidence and a wide variety of ancient non-Christian sources.[17] This has also been argued extensively by Michael Grant in *Jesus: An Historian's Review of the Gospels*.[18] Given this evidence, it is reasonable that we would accept the data about Jesus that are given to us in the Gospels.

Statement (2) is also important for our rationale. The Gospels tell us many other things about the life of Jesus, but for our purposes these four points are most essential. Again, Jesus claimed (a) to be the divine Son of God (Jn 10:30-33; 14:9; Mt 27:43; Mk 14:61-62); (b) he would be crucified and raised on the third day (Mt 16:21; 17:22-23; 20:18-19; Mk 8:31; 9:31-32); (c) the Old Testament was the Word of God (Jn 10:35; Mt 22:31; Mk 7:9-13); and (d) the Holy Spirit would guide the apostles in all truth, teach them things beyond what Jesus taught them and call to memory all he taught them (Jn 14:26; 16:13). These are just a few of the things that Jesus believed and taught. If it turns out that he is the Son of God, then each one of these beliefs finds strong support from him, and we are rational for believing them.

This brings us to statement (3), which considers some of the events surrounding Jesus' life and death. These events include that (a) Jesus was crucified, dead and buried (Mt 17:45-61; Lk 23:44-56); (b) the disciples were cowards both before and after Jesus' death (Mk 14:54, 66-72; Lk 24:1-12); (c) the tomb was well-known and well-guarded (Mt 27:62-66); (d) three days later, the tomb was empty (Mt 28:1-8; Mk 16:1-8; Jn 20:1-10); (e) Jesus reappeared to various believers and non-believers after the tomb was empty (Jn 20:11-29; 1 Cor 15:7; Acts 9:1-19); and (f) the disciples were radically transformed after seeing Jesus alive again (Acts 2:14-39; 4:1-31; 5:22-32). The facts recounted here represent the facts that any theory about Jesus' death and the events that follow must explain. This brings us to statement (4).

Statement (4) claims that Jesus rose from the dead. Skeptics may argue that other theories might explain the empty tomb and the appearances of Jesus Christ. We readily admit that there are other theories, but they all try to offer naturalistic, or at least non-miraculous, explanations for

---

[17]Gary Habermas, *The Historical Jesus: Ancient Evidence for the Life of Christ* (Joplin, MO: College Press, 1996).

[18]Michael Grant, *Jesus: An Historian's Review of the Gospels* (New York: Scribner, 1995).

these events. Over the centuries, skeptics have offered the swoon theory, wrong tomb theory, hallucination theory and the stolen body theory as possible explanations for these events. Space does not allow us to explore these rival theories, but suffice it to say that none of them hold up to the evidence and are therefore either impossible or so implausible that they should be rejected.[19]

To illustrate how these theories fail to hold up to the evidence, let us consider one example: the stolen body theory. Given the fact that this theory dates back to the first century itself (Mt 27:62-64; 28:11-15), we consider this to be the most serious challenge to the resurrection. According to this theory, Jesus' body was merely stolen by someone, and this is why the tomb was empty. But this does not seem to fit with the evidence. We must remember that the Jews and the Romans did not want Christianity to take root. The fastest way to kill this new movement would be to show people Jesus' body and that he was still dead. Thus, if the Romans or the Jews had stolen the body, then they would have quickly displayed it for all to see when reports of Jesus's resurrection began to emerge. Thus, it is safe to say that the disciples were the only likely candidates to steal the body. But how would the disciples have been able to get past the guards, and how do we then explain their willingness to endure persecution and even death for preaching Christ if they had stolen the body? If they had stolen the body, then this means they knew their preaching was a lie. It is incredibly difficult to imagine that one person, let alone a dozen people, would be willing to die for something they knew was untrue. This theory is implausible because it does not give a realistic account of the evidence that must be taken into account. If, however, we reject this view, then we are left with the resurrection of Jesus Christ. Many skeptics and critics will not like this conclusion because it is a supernatural explanation that flies in the face of their larger naturalistic worldview. But if this is the only theory that properly accounts for the events surrounding Jesus' death, then it is a conclusion we must accept.

---

[19]Numerous works exist that show the weaknesses of these theories. For a short sample, see Habermas, *Historical Jesus*, or Michael R. Licona, *The Resurrection of Jesus* (Downers Grove, IL: InterVarsity Press, 2010).

This now brings us to our conclusion: (5) Jesus is the Son of God. We come to this conclusion for two reasons. First, Jesus claimed that he would be crucified and rise the third day. The resurrection shows that Jesus fulfilled what he taught and said. Second, by coming back to life after being dead for three days, we see that Jesus has power over not only life and death but also nature in the physical world. In short, Jesus has supernatural power, and this is something that can be attributed only to God. Therefore, the resurrection shows Jesus to be the divine Son of God.

Now, if Jesus is the Son of God, then what does this mean for our belief in special revelation? First, whether or not Jesus' life reveals anything to us about God depends on whether or not he is the Son of God. So, if the resurrection shows that he is the Son of God, then the incarnation reveals something about God to us in a special way, and our belief in special revelation is a rational belief. Second, if Jesus is the Son of God, then we must pay special attention to what he believed and taught. He believed that the Old Testament was the Word of God, and he taught that the Holy Spirit would guide the apostles in all truth, teach them things beyond what he taught them and bring his teachings to their remembrance. Although this does not yield an absolute proof that the Bible is God's Word, it does at least demonstrate that people are rational and within their epistemic rights to believe that God has revealed himself in the Bible.

Conclusion

In this chapter we have considered the important matter of divine revelation. We have distinguished between natural revelation and special revelation and have argued that a religious believer is rational in believing that God has revealed himself in these two ways. These considerations do not yield absolute certainty, but they do show why these beliefs are reasonable. In the next chapter, we deal with the question of certainty.

DISCUSSION QUESTIONS

1. What are the two kinds of revelation Christianity affirms?

2. What is natural revelation, and how does it make natural theology possible?

3. What kinds of objections have been leveled against natural theology, and what reasons do we have for thinking it is possible to do?

4. What is special revelation, and what are the two forms in which it has been given?

5. What reason do we have for thinking that God has revealed himself to us through Christ and the Bible?

10

How Certain Can We Be?

JUST HOW CERTAIN CAN WE BE about what we think we know? This is a question that most students of epistemology find important. There are many things that we have great confidence about and never doubt. For example, I am highly confident that I exist, have feelings of various types and am interested in epistemological questions like these. As Descartes has noted for us, any doubt I might have about these kinds of beliefs requires that I exist to have such doubt in the first place. Yet, there are also many ideas and beliefs for which we have great uncertainty and doubt. For example, I cannot be certain that the person next to me is telling me the truth, that he is who he says he is or that he is trustworthy.

In a perfect world, we would have absolute certainty about everything we claim to know. Religious believers would have no doubts, scientists would never have to alter their theories because they would get things right the first time, and philosophers would be able to solve the great questions about reality with perfect clarity and precision. But we do not live in that world. Believers sometimes have doubts about things, scientists regularly alter their theories, and philosophers are always debating. Yet, this does not mean that we have no knowledge whatsoever or that we must be completely skeptical about all knowledge claims. Despite whatever uncertainty we might have about some things, it is also true that we have high levels of confidence in many of our beliefs. To answer the question about how certain we can be about what we think we know, this chapter will explore the issues of skepticism and dogmatism (assumption of absolute certainty) as they identify two polar opposite per-

spectives about our ability to be sure. Let us consider skepticism first and
then move on to think about the issue of certainty.

What Do Skeptics Believe?

Skepticism comes in different forms and in various degrees. In general,
however, skeptics are highly suspicious of the knowledge claims made
by others. But despite whatever negative connotations the word *skeptic*
might have, there are some healthy, or even helpful, forms of skepticism.
And while other forms of skepticism may be highly problematic, they
might still be helpful in pointing out the potential challenges we face in
our pursuit of epistemic assurance.

Common-sense skepticism is a natural and healthy form of skepticism that most of us employ on a daily basis. In this version, skeptics
question claims that are rightly questionable—like a corrupt politician's
promises—but do not subject normal beliefs or common-sense beliefs
to continual doubt. In other words, they do not question everyday oc-
currences, events or basic ideas that are obviously true. For these kinds
of beliefs and claims, skeptics take them as given and go on living normally. Some examples might help make this clear. Occasionally we find
ourselves in the market for a new car, television, insurance policy, re-
tirement plan, or something else along these lines. In these cases, we go
to the local retailer and look for the product that fits our needs the best.
We quickly realize that buying a new car is not as simple as we thought
it would be. For one thing, there are so many models, options and deal-
erships that have to be considered. And, what is most unfortunate, it is
often difficult to know if the salesperson is being honest. Or consider the
way politicians try to sell us on voting for them by making amazing
promises during their campaign. Whether buying a new car or voting
for a president, we often find ourselves skeptical of what we hear. Is this
bad? No! In fact, given the way people often lie to get what they want, it
is essential. This is what we might call common-sense skepticism. Yet,
this kind of skepticism is not our concern here. Rather, our concern is
with the different philosophical forms of skepticism that have developed
over the last few hundred years. Philosophical versions of skepticism are
much more radical in nature. In general, they either reject all knowledge

claims about physical and metaphysical things, or they reject knowledge claims about metaphysical things.

Philosophically speaking, there are numerous versions of skepticism, and, unfortunately for the philosophy student, there is little consensus on how they might be categorized. Yet, most if not all forms of skepticism fall into one of two categories: *global skepticism* or *local skepticism*. Global skeptics are skeptical of all knowledge claims of any kind. In other words, they question anyone who claims to know anything about something about a given topic. For global skeptics, it does not matter if a person is making a physical or a metaphysical claim. Their skepticism is applied to all realms of human knowledge. Local skeptics, by contrast, only question knowledge claims of a particular kind—metaphysical claims.

Methodological skepticism. Methodological skepticism employs skepticism in its attempt to gain knowledge but is not skeptical in its conclusions. In this approach, the skeptic uses doubt to weed out all the ideas that are not certain and sure. Once all these ideas have been removed, the clearest, most certain ideas which remain can be affirmed without any reasonable hesitation. Descartes, whom we will consider in a moment, is a classic example of this approach. What is important to note here is that this kind of skeptic applies skepticism globally—that is, to all knowledge claims—in an effort to identify those claims which are obviously and necessarily true. Yet, despite the global application of skepticism in their methodology, this form of skepticism is not as radical as some other forms of skepticism because these skeptics are often quite willing to make knowledge claims of various kinds.

Metaphysical skepticism. This form of skepticism suggests that we can have knowledge of the natural world via science and sense perceptions. But it denies the possibility of gaining any knowledge of the metaphysical realm or metaphysical things. So, for example, it suggests that we can have knowledge of stars, apples, gravity, cardiovascular systems, social structures and economic patterns but holds that we cannot know anything about God, souls or goodness. In other words, to say that we can know nothing about these things means that we cannot know what they are like or if they even exist. In contrast to methodological skepticism, which applies skepticism globally, this form of skepticism is local in that it focuses its criticisms on only one kind of knowledge claim. Despite this, however, this kind of skepticism is a bit more radical than its methodological counterpart, because it denies our ability to make certain kinds of knowledge claims.

Pyrrhonian skepticism. Pyrrhonian skepticism is the most radical form of skepticism and is generally what people have in mind when they hear the word *skeptic.* This view argues that we do not have any knowledge or that we should suspend all judgments about our knowledge due to various factors that make knowledge impossible. This approach is similar to methodological skepticism, because it is skeptical of all knowledge claims, whether physical or metaphysical. But it is unlike the methodological approach in the kinds of conclusions that it draws. While the methodological approach is willing to grant various kinds of knowledge claims, the Pyrrhonian approach is not. For this kind of skeptic, both physical and metaphysical knowledge claims cannot be granted.

Here we should also note that this version of skepticism can take a harder or a softer approach, depending on the philosopher in question. The harder Pyrrhonian skeptics are often referred to as unmitigated skeptics, and the softer advocates are often called mitigated skeptics. Unmitigated skeptics claim that definitely and dogmatically they know that no one knows anything. This is obviously self-defeating. Mitigated skeptics simply believe that no one knows anything.

WHO WERE THE IMPORTANT SKEPTICAL PHILOSOPHERS?

So, who were the important skeptical philosophers? History shows that there have been quite a number of them. Yet, a small sample will suffice for our purposes here. Let us consider a few from the ancient and the modern world.

Pyrrho of Ellis. Pyrrho of Ellis (360–270 B.C.) is one of the most important ancient skeptical philosophers. Like later skeptics who would bear his name (the Pyrrhonians), Pyrrho was a global skeptic who was unwilling to accept any knowledge claim as true. Diogenes Laertius (third century A.D.) summarizes Pyrrho's teachings. He says:

> The sceptics [Pyrrhonians], then, spent their time overturning all the
> dogmas of the schools, whereas they themselves make no dogmatic pro-

nouncements, and while they presented and set out in detail the views of others, they themselves expressed no determinate opinions, not even this itself [that they had no determinate opinion]. Thus, they even abolished the position of holding no determinate opinion, saying, for example, "we determine nothing" since otherwise they would be determining something.[1]

For Pyrrho, then, it was best to withhold judgment and avoid making any knowledge claims whatsoever.

Sextus Empiricus. Another important ancient skeptical philosopher was Sextus Empiricus (A.D. 160–210). Sextus took Pyrrho's skepticism and added his own twist to it. For him, skepticism was motivated out of a desire for peace. In his mind, disturbances happen in our lives as we try to determine which view of something is the correct view. And because, according to Sextus, any good argument for something can be opposed by an equally strong counterargument, the seeker of truth will be constantly plagued by doubt and unrest. His solution was to denounce all knowledge claims. He says, "The sceptical ability is the ability to set in opposition appearances and ideas in any manner whatsoever, the result of which is first that, because of the equal force of the opposed objects and arguments, final suspension of judgment is achieved, and then freedom from disturbance."[2] He then went on to say, "We say most definitely that the goal of the sceptic is the freedom from disturbance with respect to matters of belief and also moderate states with respect to things that are matters of compulsion."[3]

René Descartes. One important version of philosophical skepticism emerged in the seventeenth century with Descartes. Though not ultimately a skeptic himself, Descartes did employ systematic doubt about all beliefs to identify those ideas which were undoubtable. Descartes illustrates methodological skepticism. He says, "I thought it necessary to . . . reject as absolutely false everything in which I could imagine the slightest doubt and to see, as a result, if anything remained among my beliefs that was completely indubitable. Thus, because our senses some-

---

[1]Diogenes Laertius, "Life of Pyrrho," in *Hellenistic Philosophy*, trans. Brad Inwood and L. P. Gerson (Indianapolis: Hackett, 1997), 288.
[2]Sextus Empiricus, "General Principles," in *Hellenistic Philosophy*, trans. Brad Inwood and L. P. Gerson (Indianapolis: Hackett, 1997), 303.
[3]Ibid., 307.

times deceive us, I decided to assume that nothing was the way the senses made us imagine it."[4]

First-year philosophy students often find it odd that a man searching for certainty would begin with such radical and systematic doubt. But after a little reflection, one can understand why he might approach his task this way. Descartes noted that it is at least within the realm of possibility that an evil demon exists which deceives us about all our perceptions and knowledge claims. If it is possible that this demon exists, then it would seem that we can be certain of nothing whatsoever. Descartes felt that to overcome this concern, one must be willing to explore the possibility to see if there is anything we can know for sure.

And so, Descartes subjected all of his beliefs to radical, systematic doubt. But by so doing, he quickly found that there was at least one thing that was clear, distinct and indubitable: his own existence. While he could doubt the physical objects around him that present themselves to us through the senses, he could not doubt the existence of his own mind. For if he was doubting it, he was thinking to doubt it, and if he was thinking, then he must exist to think in the first place. This idea, for Descartes, was absolutely certain and sure and could thus serve as the foundational idea on which to build all other knowledge. From this foundational idea, Descartes went on to argue for the existence of God, who would not, due to his goodness, allow us to be continually deceived by an evil demon. If this is true, then we can once again be confident in our perceptual abilities and our ability to reason, as long as we do so properly. In the end, Descartes was not a skeptic. Epistemologically speaking, he began with global, methodological skepticism in order to find clear and distinct ideas that serve as the foundation for the rest of his knowledge.

David Hume. As we saw in chapter 3, Hume divided all knowledge claims into two categories: (1) relations of ideas and (2) matters of fact. Knowledge claims based on the relations of ideas are statements whose predicates are already present within the subject. For example, statements like "Triangles have three sides" or "Bachelors are unmarried" fall

---

[4]René Descartes, *Discourse on Method* (Indianapolis: Hackett, 1998), 24.

into this category. In both cases, the subjects of each statement already contain the information given in the last part of the statement. After all, by definition, triangles have three sides to them. We do not need the phrase "have three sides" in order to know what a triangle is. The same is true with the second claim. Bachelors are by definition unmarried. Statements of fact are different in that the predicates of these statements tell us something new about the subject. For example, "The ball is red" is a matter of fact. The subject "ball" does not contain the idea of being "red." So, in this statement, we learn something new about the particular ball in question. Hume's dividing of knowledge claims into these two categories is often referred to as Hume's fork.

According to Hume, knowledge is possible only if it comes in one of these two forms—relations of ideas or matter of fact. While much of our empirical knowledge falls within these two categories, Hume argued that metaphysical claims do not. And because of this, he thought that all metaphysical claims were baseless and should be rejected. This led Hume to reject that we can know a number of ideas that most of us take for granted. For example, Hume said we could not know the principle of causality. This principle states that every effect has a cause. The idea of causality is universally recognized, as we observe it regularly in the world. I accidentally knock a glass over on the table in front of me. If we ask, "What caused the glass to fall over?" the reply would obviously be, "You hit it." Hume analyzed the idea of causality and said there were three necessary elements to any causal event: contiguity (contact), priority in time (the cause occurs before the event) and a necessary connection between the contact and the event. Hume said we observe only two of these elements: contact and priority. We cannot observe the necessary connection. We naturally assume such a connection, but we do not observe it. The connection is neither a relation of ideas nor a matter of fact. Therefore we cannot claim to know it.[5] Hume argued in a similar fashion against knowledge of such things as the mind or soul, the idea

---

[5]It is important to note that Hume never denied causality itself. In a 1754 letter to John Stewart he stated that he "never asserted so absurd a proposition as that something could arise without a cause. I only maintained that our certainty of Falsehood of the proposition proceeded neither from intuition nor demonstration but from another source." David Hume, *The Letters of David Hume*, 2 vols., ed. J. Y. T. Grieg (Oxford: Clarendon, 1932), 1:187.

of substance and the existence of God. He famously said:

> When we run over our libraries, persuaded of these principles, what havoc must we make? If we take in our hand any volume of divinity or school metaphysics, of instance, let us ask, does it contain an abstract reasoning concerning quantity or number? No. Does it contain any experimental reasoning concerning matter of fact and existence? No. Commit it then to the flames: for it can contain nothing but sophistry and illusion.[6]

Immanuel Kant. Another classic example of a skeptic is Immanuel Kant (1724–1804). Specifically, Kant is a prime example of metaphysical skepticism. For Kant, knowledge required (1) sense data and (2) an active mind to process, arrange and structure the sense data. But if Kant is right about this, then it would be impossible to gain knowledge with any sense perceptions of a given entity. And because we normally do not have direct access to God via the senses, this would mean that it is impossible to have knowledge of God and the metaphysical realm. Kant went to great lengths to show how it is possible to gain knowledge of the physical realm (an argument far too complex for our purposes here) but argues that metaphysical knowledge is impossible. He says:

> Respecting these sciences, as they do certainly exist, it may with propriety be asked, *how* they are possible?—for that they must be possible, is shown by the fact of their really existing. But as to metaphysics, the miserable progress it has hitherto made, and the fact that of no one system yet brought forward, as far as regard its true aim, can it be said that this science really exists leaves anyone at liberty to doubt with reason the very possibility of its existence.[7]

This does not, however, mean that Kant thought God cannot, or does not, exist. While Kant believed one could not justify a belief in the existence of God on the basis of pure reason, he did believe that one could justify belief on the basis of practical reason. In his *Critique of Practical Reason,* Kant stated, "Two things fill the mind with ever-increasing admiration and awe—the starry heavens above me and the moral law

---

[6]David Hume, *An Enquiry Concerning Human Understanding* (New York: Cambridge University Press, 2007), 165.

[7]Immanuel Kant, *Critique of Pure Reason*, trans. J. M. D. Meiklejohn (Amherst, NY: Prometheus, 1990), 13.

within me."[8] Kant was convinced of the existence of absolute moral laws. He argued that God must exist in order for such laws to make sense. For if good does not win over evil in the end, then moral duties make no sense. One needs an absolute, good, all-powerful being to guarantee that good wins in the end. Hence, for practical reasons, there must be a God. In other words, he thought that we can talk about God and are justified in believing in him for practical considerations, but we can never have knowledge about him on the basis of pure reason.

WHAT CAUSES SKEPTICISM?

Most of us find it odd to hear radical skeptics denying everything we think we know. It is natural to wonder why philosophers would come to these conclusions. The reasons vary from philosopher to philosopher, but we can identify some of the common concerns of these philosophers over the years.

First, many philosophers have had great concerns with our perceptual limitations. As we noted in chapter 6 when dealing with the issue of perception, it is often the case that we think we see or perceive one thing, only to find out that we are seeing things incorrectly. For example, while driving my car I might think I see a dead dog in the road off in the distance. But, as I drive closer to the black object in the road, I begin to realize that it is not a dead dog. I now believe it is a black suitcase that has fallen out of someone's car. But as I get closer still, I come to see that it is a large piece of tire debris that has come from an eighteen-wheeler. In my earliest perceptual moments of the object, I was misled by my senses. Or consider the way earlier civilizations thought that the earth was flat. For many people, that was a reasonable belief to hold given their perceptions of flat horizons all around them. These cases remind us that our senses might be wrong about the way things are. If so, then one can understand why one would be skeptical.

Second, some philosophers have also noted that reason can lead us astray. Kant, for example, strongly criticized the use of reason alone to secure metaphysical knowledge. Despite what many other philosophers

---

[8]Immanuel Kant, *Critique of Practical Reason*, trans. Thomas Kingsmill Abbott (Hazelton, PA: Pennsylvania State University Electronic Classic Series, 2010), 128.

had said, he suggested that reason would never be sufficient to show that God exists, because it is possible to make good reasonable arguments for and against God's existence. In his view, this explained why philosophy, or at least metaphysics, had made virtually no progress before him. Moreover, some philosophers have noted that our reasoning is not as objective as we might think it is. In the Enlightenment, for example, philosophers thought that we could be completely objective in our perspectives and see things directly as they are. But more recently, postmodern philosophers have noted the sociological influences that shape the way we perceive and think. And because of this, our reasoning is affected by subjective factors.

Third, other philosophers have assumed that knowledge requires absolute certainty in order to be counted as knowledge. And because certainty has been so elusive, they suggest that it is impossible to know anything for sure. Consider a few popular examples of the kinds of things that we cannot be certain about. How can I be sure, for example, that I am not just a brain in a vat of fluid with electrodes stimulating my brain to make me think I am sitting here typing this chapter? Though this question seems absurd and virtually no one thinks this is the case, I cannot prove with certainty that it is not really the case. Or, how can I be sure that there are other minds in this world? After all, this too could be an illusion in my own mind. And even though we believe in the existence of other minds with full confidence, we still cannot prove that something like this is untrue. In the end, we must admit that even things we take to be real and true cannot be established with absolute certainty. These are a few of the reasons that philosophers have argued for skepticism.

What Is Wrong with Skepticism?

So, what should we think about skepticism? Should we throw our hands in the air with the skeptics and think that we know nothing or should suspend all judgments about knowledge claims? Ultimately, the more radical versions of skepticism are a dead-end street and seem to be intellectually implausible. But this does not mean that there is nothing of value in skeptical thought. As we noted earlier, all of us exercise common-sense skepticism on a daily basis, and we avoid major problems because of this. But even the philosophical versions have some benefit. If nothing else, they remind us of the need for epistemic humility. It is an all too common fault for persons to make assertions about issues of which they often have little knowledge or evidence. Recently I (Foreman) had an encounter with a young man who claimed, "I'm an atheist, and I believe all religions are fairy tales made up by people who just want power over others and believed in by people who are too weak-minded to confront the realities of life without the mental security blanket of an imaginary all-powerful being who cares and looks after them even when things are bad." It seems that this young man could use a healthy dose of epistemic humility, because he had no evidence to justify any of these claims. Skepticism reminds us to be careful about overstating our case for the beliefs we hold.

Nevertheless, there are good reasons for rejecting skepticism. First, much of skeptical thought is either self-defeating or impractical. Consider the unmitigated skeptic's claim that "I know that no one has any knowledge." To say that it is impossible to have knowledge is itself a knowledge claim, and thus this position is self-defeating. Furthermore, this approach is contradicted by our actions, because no one lives this way. Our lives require knowledge of many different things in order to function properly, and yet, for the most part, we manage to live our lives quite well. How is this possible if we know nothing about the way things are? Thus, unmitigated skepticism is highly problematic. But what about mitigated skeptics who simply *believe* that it is impossible to have knowledge? This approach might be less obviously self-defeating than unmitigated skepticism, but it still has problems. Suppose we were to ask a mitigated skeptic, "Do you know that you believe no one knows anything?" In order to avoid the self-defeating error of the unmitigated skeptic, he might reply, "No, but I believe it." But then we could ask, "Do you know that you believe it?" He may continue to claim that he does not know, he just believes, but now he has a problem because he has no ultimate basis for his belief. He ends up in an infinite regression of belief claims without ever being able to justify any of them. So, mitigated skepticism is just as problematic as unmitigated skepticism.

Second, despite the occasional perceptual difficulties we might have, there are good reasons to think that we do have knowledge of the world. While it is true that we can be misled by our senses, it is also true that they give us good information more often than not. Take, for example, the information you get from your eyes as you drive down the road in your car. Suppose you are driving down a two-lane road—one lane going north, and the other going south—and a massive eighteen-wheeler is approaching you. Both you and the eighteen-wheeler are traveling at about sixty-five to seventy miles per hour, and as the truck gets closer to you, you notice that it swerves into your lane. What do you do at this moment? Do you pause for a time of reflection about the reliability of your senses—wondering whether or not you can trust the information they are giving you—or do you hit the brakes and swerve? You swerve! But why do you do this? You do it because failing to do so would cause you—and any loved ones you have in the car with you—to be killed. Skeptics raise good philosophical points for us and remind us that we can make errors in our thinking. But suggesting that we cannot trust our senses is both dangerous and foolish. The fact is, as the case of the swerving eighteen-wheeler reminds us, our senses give us important information about the world that is, in most cases, true. We are also reminded of this when we consider the progress of the natural sciences over the past few centuries. Because of this progress, we now have the ability to do open-heart surgery, put people on the moon and fly around the world in less than twenty-four hours. How is any of this possible if our senses tell us nothing about the world?

Third, skeptics have raised important considerations about the possibility of having metaphysical knowledge. But their criticisms overstate the case. It is true that getting this kind of knowledge is difficult. But difficult does not mean impossible. In recent philosophy, there has been a resurgence of metaphysical discussion by both believers and nonbelievers. We now recognize that certain scientific and mathematical inquiries thrust us directly into the domain of metaphysics. This may indeed be a chastened approach to metaphysics, but it is metaphysics nonetheless. Moreover, as we noted in chapter 9, having some form of divine revelation makes metaphysical knowledge a possibility.

Finally, skepticism implies that knowledge requires absolute certainty.

However, this expectation sets the bar too high and is unrealistic. As W. Jay Wood puts it:

> The strict demands for unimpeachable certainty leave one with so small a set of basic beliefs that they can't possibly bear the heavy weight of all that we believe. A moment's reflection shows that the thousands of beliefs we hold about matters aesthetic, moral, religious, political, economic, historical, scientific, philosophical and so on can't all be derived from the very small set of basic beliefs insisted on by strong foundationalists.[9]

If certainty is required, then skepticism has a much stronger case. But if certainty is not required, then skepticism is weak. We might not have an absolute certainty about many things, but this does not mean that we know nothing about them whatsoever. So the next question is, "Do we need certainty in order to have knowledge?"

WHAT IS REASONABLE TO HOPE FOR?

In the last section we noted that skepticism goes too far. Despite what difficulties we might have, we still have knowledge of various kinds. But does this mean that we have certainty about what we claim to know? Unfortunately, it does not. Even if skepticism goes too far, it still reminds us that we have some epistemic limitations. The fact is that we sometimes fail to understand things the way they are. This can happen because our senses fail us, we have a lack of relevant data or we reason incorrectly. But these are not the only factors that make certainty so elusive. It is also the case that we are finite creatures trying to wrap our minds around things that are complex and difficult. At times, our finite minds are unable to go as far as we would like to go.

In addition to this, it is possible that our perspective on a given issue is unduly influenced by social factors. That is, although we think of ourselves as being objective about our views, things are not that simple. Our view is often influenced by various social, religious, historical and cultural factors. As Daniel Taylor notes, "We belong to communities of belief which help shape, whether we are conscious of it or not, our views

---

[9]W. Jay Wood, *Epistemology: Becoming Intellectually Virtuous* (Downers Grove, IL: InterVarsity Press, 1998), 94-95.

of the world and our actions in it. We both draw from these communities and contribute to them, the reflective and the unreflective alike. They help determine what we are."[10] Alan Padgett argues the same point, saying, "None of us has a God's-eye view, a 'view from nowhere.' Any approach that hopes to grasp the object of our studies will need a host of contrasting, alternative points of view on that object."[11]

So then, if skepticism goes too far in one direction by calling all knowledge claims into question, but it is still impossible to have absolute certainty about much of what we claim to know, then what would a reasonable epistemic expectation be for us regarding our knowledge? How sure can we expect to be? In general, we suggest that the answer lies somewhere in the middle. That is, we contend that certainty—for most things—should never be our goal. In most cases, we can attain great levels of confidence or assurance about our beliefs, but not absolute certainty. Accepting, or assuming, the standard of absolute epistemic certainty for our knowledge claims leads to the ridiculous position that we know nothing whatsoever, or almost nothing. Esther Lightcap Meek puts it this way: "The ideal of certainty in knowledge is this: I must accept as true only those claims of which I am rationally certain, having no shadow of doubt. The search for such certainty, we have found in the centuries of our Western tradition, has led the stalwart to part with even the dearest of the commitments to which we might be naturally inclined."[12] She then adds, "Driven to attain an ideal of certainty, thinkers have over the centuries tightened the parameters of 'proper' knowledge so restrictively that what was left was at best truisms, or so minimalistic and private that all the mess of reality has been squeezed out of them."[13]

This does not mean that we cannot have certainty about some things. It simply means that most of our beliefs and knowledge claims do not reach this level. Yet, Alister McGrath notes that we generally regard the kinds of things that we have certainty about as being relatively

---

[10]Daniel Taylor, *The Myth of Certainty: The Reflective Christian and the Risk of Commitment* (Downers Grove, IL: InterVarsity Press, 1992), 21.

[11]Alan G. Padgett, *Science and the Study of God* (Grand Rapids: Eerdmans, 2003), 24.

[12]Esther Lightcap Meek, *Longing to Know: The Philosophy of Knowledge for Ordinary People* (Grand Rapids: Brazos Press, 2003), 32.

[13]Ibid., 33.

unimportant to our lives. By contrast, those things that are important to us are the things that we cannot be completely sure about. He says:

> The beliefs that are really important in life concern such things as whether there is a God and what he is like, or the mystery of human nature and destiny. These—and a whole host of other important beliefs—have two basic features. In the first place, they are *relevant* to life. They matter, in that they affect the way we think, live, hope and act. In the second place, by their very nature they make claims that *cannot be proved* (or disproved) with total certainty. At best we may hope to know them as probably true. There will always be an element of doubt in any statement that goes beyond the world of logic and self-evident propositions. Christianity is not unique in this respect: an atheist or Marxist is confronted with precisely the same dilemma.[14]

Garrett DeWeese makes a similar point, saying, "The stock of propositions about which I can have certainty is not all that large; most of the really interesting things that I believe in life are such that I recognize that I *could* possibly be wrong about them."[15]

This raises an important point that needs to be considered briefly. There are a few things that we can have certainty about, but for most things, certainty eludes us. This suggests that there are various degrees or levels of assurance that we can have. At the highest level, one might have what we call *logical* or *absolute certainty*. This is the kind of certainty that makes a belief impossible to doubt. These include, as McGrath notes, logical statements, self-evident truths or many mathematical propositions. For example, $2 + 2 = 4$ or "All triangles have three sides" fall into this category. These are statements that could not possibly be untrue. After this, there is a level of assurance that we might call *probabilistic certainty*. These include statements like "The sun will rise tomorrow" or "The pen will fall if I drop it." These statements are considered to be true by everyone. But it is always possible that the sun will not rise tomorrow or that the pen could float on this one occasion. One cannot claim to know with certainty that these things will happen. Nevertheless, it is

---

[14]Alister E. McGrath, *Doubting* (Downers Grove, IL: InterVarsity Press, 2006), 24-25.
[15]Garrett J. DeWeese, *Doing Philosophy as a Christian* (Downers Grove, IL: InterVarsity Press, 2011), 158.

foolish to think that these things might not happen given the universal track record of the sun coming up and of gravity pulling pens to the floor. There is also what we might call *sufficient certainty*. In this case, we have very good evidence in favor of a particular belief and know of no significant defeaters for this belief.

But if there are varying degrees of certainty, what causes this variation? Again, McGrath is helpful here. He notes that the degrees of certainty arise from the nature of the objects, entities or issues that we inquire about. In other words, the nature of the thing in question largely determines how it can be known. So, for example, when we are asking about apples, we use our senses to investigate them and see what they are like. By contrast, when we are asking questions about God, who cannot be seen with our eyes or touched with our hands, we must rely on something different. In this, we see how the nature of the object determines how we know it. But, as McGrath notes, the nature of the object also determines how well it can be known. He says, "The degree of theoretical [certainty] that may be secured for any aspect of reality is determined by its intrinsic nature. We are thus obliged to think in terms of a range of possibilities of closure, depending on which stratum of reality is being encountered and represented in this manner."[16] In other words, we may know some things more directly and as they appear more obvious to us. This does not suggest any kind of superiority or deficiency in the objects themselves. It simply recognizes certain epistemological facts about the way our minds apprehend reality and the limitations of our cognitive processes.

Conclusion

In this chapter we have surveyed a wide range of perspectives on the amount of assurance we have regarding our knowledge. Skepticism raises important questions about our cognitive and perceptual limitations but goes too far and leaves us with nothing, or almost nothing, that can be known. In the end, there are good reasons for thinking that we can have varying degrees of knowledge about the world.

---

[16]Alister E. McGrath, *The Science of God: An Introduction to Scientific Theology* (Grand Rapids: Eerdmans, 2004), 187. McGrath uses the word *closure*, and we have substituted the word *certainty* here, as this is what McGrath has in view.

DISCUSSION QUESTIONS

1. In general, what do skeptics believe?

2. What does methodological skepticism affirm, and whose view is a good example of this?

3. How is metaphysical skepticism similar to and different from methodological skepticism?

4. What is Pyrrhonian skepticism, and what makes it unique?

5. What reasons are there for thinking that skepticism is not adequate?

6. Regarding certainty and assurance, what is a reasonable expectation?

For Further Reading

GENERAL EPISTEMOLOGY

Audi, Robert. *Epistemology: A Contemporary Introduction to the Theory of Knowledge*. New York: Routledge, 1998.

Chisholm, Roderick M. *The Foundations of Knowing*. Minneapolis: University of Minnesota, 1982.

Crumley II, Jack S. *An Introduction to Epistemology*. Mountain View, CA: Mayfield, 1999.

Dancy, Jonathan. *Introduction to Contemporary Epistemology*. Malden, MA: Blackwell, 1985.

Meek, Esther Lightcap. *Longing to Know: The Philosophy of Knowledge for Ordinary People*. (Grand Rapids: Brazos Press, 2003).

_____. *Loving to Know: Covenant Epistemology*. Eugene, OR: Cascade, 2011.

Moser, Paul K., Dwayne H. Mulder and J. D. Trout. *The Theory of Knowledge: A Thematic Introduction*. New York: Oxford University Press, 1998.

Pojman, Louis P. *What Can We Know? An Introduction to the Theory of Knowledge*. Belmont, CA: Wadsworth, 2001.

Pritchard, Duncan. *What Is This Thing Called Knowledge?* New York: Routledge, 2006.

Zagzebski, Linda Trinkaus. *On Epistemology*. Belmont, CA: Wadsworth, 2009.

CLASSICAL READINGS

Aristotle. *The Complete Works of Aristotle*. Edited by Jonathan Barnes. 2 vols. Princeton, NJ: Princeton University Press, 1984.

Descartes, René. *Discourse on Method*. Translated by Desmond M. Clarke. London: Penguin, 1999.

_____. *Meditations on First Philosophy*. Translated by Donald A. Cress. 4th ed. Indianapolis: Hackett, 1998.

Hume, David. *Enquiries Concerning Human Understanding and Concerning the Principles of Morals.* 3rd ed. Oxford: Clarendon Paperbacks, Clarendon Press, 1975.

_____. *The Natural History of Religion.* Edited by H. E. Root. Palo Alto, CA: Stanford University Press, 1957.

_____. *A Treatise of Human Nature.* London: Penguin, 1969.

Kant, Immanuel. *The Critique of Judgment.* Translated by J. H. Bernard. Amherst, NY: Prometheus, 2000.

_____. *Critique of Practical Reason.* Translated by T. K. Abbott. Amherst, NY: Prometheus, 1996.

_____. *Critique of Pure Reason.* Translated by J. M. D. Meiklejohn. Amherst, NY: Prometheus, 1990.

Locke, John. *An Essay Concerning Human Understanding.* London: Penguin, 2004.

_____. *The Reasonableness of Christianity.* Edited by I. T. Ramsey. Palo Alto, CA: Stanford University Press, 1958.

Plato. *Plato: Complete Works.* Edited by John M. Cooper. Indianapolis: Hackett, 1997.

Sources of Knowledge

Cody, C. A. J. *Testimony: A Philosophical Study.* New York: Oxford University Press, 1994.

Trout, J. D. *Measuring the Intentional World: Realism, Naturalism and Quantitative Methods in the Behavioral Sciences.* New York: Oxford University Press, 1998.

Truth

Groothuis, Douglas. *Truth Decay: Defending Christianity Against the Challenges of Postmodernism.* Downers Grove, IL: InterVarsity Press, 2000.

Kelly, Stewart E. *Truth Considered and Applied: Examining Postmodernism, History and Christian Faith.* Nashville: B&H Academic, 2011.

Köstenberger, Andreas, ed. *Whatever Happened to Truth?* Wheaton, IL: Crossway, 2005.

Inferences

Corbett, Edward P. J. *The Elements of Reasoning.* New York: Allyn & Bacon, 1991.

Holland, John H., Keith J. Holyoak, Richard E. Nisbett and Paul R. Thagard. *Induction: Process of Inference, Learning and Discovery.* Cambridge, MA: MIT

Press, 1989.

Lipton, Peter. *Inference to the Best Explanation.* New York: Routledge, 1991.

Toulmin, Stephen, Richard Rieke and Allan Janik, eds. *An Introduction to Reasoning.* New York: Macmillan, 1984.

PERCEPTION

Alston, William P. *The Reliability of Sense Perception.* Ithaca, NY: Cornell University Press, 1996.

Chisholm, Roderick M. *Perceiving: A Philosophical Study.* Ithaca, NY: Cornell University Press, 1957.

Fish, William. *Philosophy of Perception: A Contemporary Introduction.* New York: Routledge, 2010.

Hoffman, Donald D. *Visual Intelligence: How We Create What We See.* New York: W. W. Norton, 1998.

JUSTIFICATION

Alston, William P. *Beyond "Justification."* Ithaca, NY: Cornell University Press, 2005.

Plantinga, Alvin. *Warrant: The Current Debate.* New York: Oxford University Press, 1993.

_____. *Warrant and Proper Function.* New York: Oxford University Press, 1993.

_____. *Warranted Christian Belief.* New York: Oxford University Press, 2000.

Swinburne, Richard. *Epistemic Justification.* New York: Oxford University Press, 2001.

VIRTUE EPISTEMOLOGY

Baehr, Jason. *The Inquiring Mind: On Intellectual Virtues and Virtue Epistemology.* New York: Oxford University Press, 2011.

Roberts, Robert C., and W. Jay Wood, *Intellectual Virtues: An Essay in Regulative Epistemology.* New York: Oxford University Press, 2010.

Sosa, Ernest. *A Virtue Epistemology: Apt Belief and Reflective Knowledge.* New York: Oxford University Press, 2009.

Wood, W. Jay. *Epistemology: Becoming Intellectually Virtuous.* Downers Grove, IL: InterVarsity Press, 1998.

Zagzebski, Linda Trinkaus. *Virtues of the Mind: An Inquiry into the Nature of Virtue and the Ethical Foundations of Knowledge.* New York: Cambridge University Press, 1998.

Revelation

Barr, James. *Biblical Faith and Natural Theology*. New York: Oxford University Press, 1993.

Craig, William Lane, and J. P. Moreland. *The Blackwell Companion to Natural Theology*. Malden, MA: Wiley-Blackwell, 2009.

Geivett, R. Douglas, and Brendan Sweetman. *Contemporary Perspectives on Religious Epistemology*. New York: Oxford University Press, 1992.

McGrath, Alister E. *The Open Secret: A New Vision for Natural Theology*. Malden, MA: Blackwell, 2008.

Sudduth, Michael. *The Reformed Objection to Natural Theology*. Burlington, VT: Ashgate, 2009.

Skepticism and Certainty

Adler, Mortimer J. *Truth in Religion: The Plurality of Religions and the Unity of Truth*. New York: Collier, 1990.

Hiebert, Paul G. *Missiological Implications of Epistemological Shifts: Affirming Truth in a Postmodern World*. Harrisburg, PA: Trinity Press International, 1999.

Landesman, Charles, and Roblin Meeks, eds. *Philosophical Skepticism*. Malden, MA: Blackwell, 2003.

Polanyi, Michael. *Personal Knowledge: Towards a Post-Critical Philosophy*. Chicago: Chicago University Press, 1962.

Taylor, Daniel. *The Myth of Certainty: The Reflective Christian and the Risk of Commitment*. Downers Grove, IL: InterVarsity Press, 1992.

About the Authors

James K. Dew Jr. (PhD, Southeastern Baptist Theological Seminary, PhD candidate, University of Birmingham, UK) is dean of the College at Southeastern Baptist Theological Seminary in Wake Forest, North Carolina, where he is also associate professor of philosophy and the history of ideas. He is the author of *Science and Theology: Assessing Alister McGrath's Critical Realist Perspective* (Wipf & Stock), and coeditor with Chad Meister of *God and Evil: The Case for God in a World Filled with Pain* (IVP). He lives in Wake Forest with his wife and four children.

Mark W. Foreman (PhD, University of Virginia) is professor of philosophy at Liberty University in Lynchburg, Virginia. He has written numerous articles in philosophy and theology journals. He is the author of *Christianity and Bioethics* (College Press) and *Prelude to Philosophy: Critical Thinking About Basic Beliefs* (IVP).

Index

Finding the Texbook You Need

The IVP Academic Textbook Selector
is an online tool for instantly finding the IVP books
suitable for over 250 courses across 24 disciplines.

www.ivpress.com/academic/textbookselector